Dedicated to Savy and Peanut, who make every day an adventure. Thank you for traveling the world with us.

CHINA

Educational Resources, Crafts & Activities for Kids

Sarah M. Prowant, MSN-Ed, RN

Savy Activities
Colorado, USA

Savy Activities© All Rights Reserved

TERMS & CONDITIONS

This product is licensed for single use only (single home or classroom). Redistributing, selling, editing or sharing any part of this product in any part thereof is strictly forbidden without the written permission of Savy Activities. You may make copies for your personal use but will need to purchase separate licenses for use in additional classrooms and/or schools. Failure to comply is a legal copyright infringement and will be prosecuted to the full extent of the law.

When posting photos of any part of this product on social media, please give credit to "Savy Activities" by hyperlinking to our website and tagging us as @SavyActivities on social media.

We reserve the right to change this policy at any time. If you have any questions regarding this or other of our materials, please contact us directly.

FOR BEST RESULTS:

 When assembling a 3D model, glue a second piece of thick paper with a craft glue stick to back of each sheet of model pieces (prior to cutting pieces) to provide additional stability when assembled.

 Laminate all cards & posters with at least 3 ml lamination for additional protection.

 If printing from an ebook, cardstock paper (>60 lbs) provides best results for cards, models and manipulative activities, while standard printer paper is adequate for recipes, lessons, etc. Please set printer to "FIT TO PAGE" when printing for best results.

FOLLOW US ON SOCIAL MEDIA!

 @savyactivities

 /SavyActivities

www.SavyActivities.com

WHATS INCLUDED:

- Educational Placemat/Poster
- Chinese Flag
- Chinese Landmark Three-Part Cards
- Chinese Landmark Map Pinning
- China Provinces Poster
- Chinese Fun Fact Cards
- Chinese Historical Timeline Poster
- Chinese Time-Periods Connectable Cards
- Chinese Zodiac Ring Cards
- Chinese Lunar Calendar
- Great Wall of China 3D Model
- Chinese Fauna Three-Part Cards
- Life Cycle & Parts of & Tracing Giant Panda
- Panda Counting
- Tiger & Panda Masks
- "The Story of the Chinese Zodiac" Mini-book
- Traditional Chinese Clothing Dolls
- Lunar New Year Slime
- Lunar New Year Sensory Tray
- Clothespin Dragon
- Red Envelope Craft
- Chinese Ribbon Dance
- Chow Mein Recipe
- Paper Making Activity
- Chinese Paper Lanterns Craft
- Frying Pan Gong
- Chinese Currency Study: Renminbi
- Units of Measurement - Mountains
- Parts of the Mushroom Poster
- Mushroom Pileus Shapes & Cards
- Confucius Coloring Page
- Mandarin Chinese Letter Tracing
- Tangram Puzzle
- Counting Clip Cards

China

National Flora: Plum Blossoum
National Fauna: Giant Panda
Capital City: Beijing
Currency: Renminbi ¥
Language: Mandarin
National Holiday(s): February 12, Chinese New Year

Famous Landmarks:
- Great Wall
- Mount Everest
- Terracotta Warriors
- Forbidden City
- Leshan Giant Buddha
- Temple of Heaven
- Tiananmen Square
- Potala Palace

China

China Landmarks (3-Part Cards)

Great Wall

Mount Everest

Terracotta Warriors

Forbidden City

China Landmarks (3-Part Cards)

Great Wall

Mount Everest

Terracotta Warriors

Forbidden City

China Landmarks (3-Part Cards)

Leshan Giant Buddha

Temple of Heaven

Tiananmen Square

Potala Palace

China Landmarks (3-Part Cards)

Leshan Giant Buddha

Temple of Heaven

Tiananmen Square

Potala Palace

China Landmarks

Cut out circles using a 1" circle punch or scissors. Place circles on map where the landmarks are located. Refer to the control version for help if needed.

China Cities

Cut out the labels and attach them to the diagram

| Beijing | Shanghai | Hong Kong | Taipei |

| Guangzhou | Nanjing | Chongping | Tianjin |

| Shenzhen |

| Chengdu |

| Lhasa |

| Dongguan |

Instructions

Paste included map illustration onto foamboard, cardboard or corkboard. Glue straight or T-pin to back of labels or photo circles and pin into map at appropriate location of landmark or city.

China

Beijing
Tianjin

Nanjing
Shanghai

Taipei

Guangzhou   Dongguan
Shenzhen
Hong Kong

Chengdu
Chongping

Lhasa

*Please note that the locations may not be exact as markers are positioned to be seen when multiple locations are in similar area.

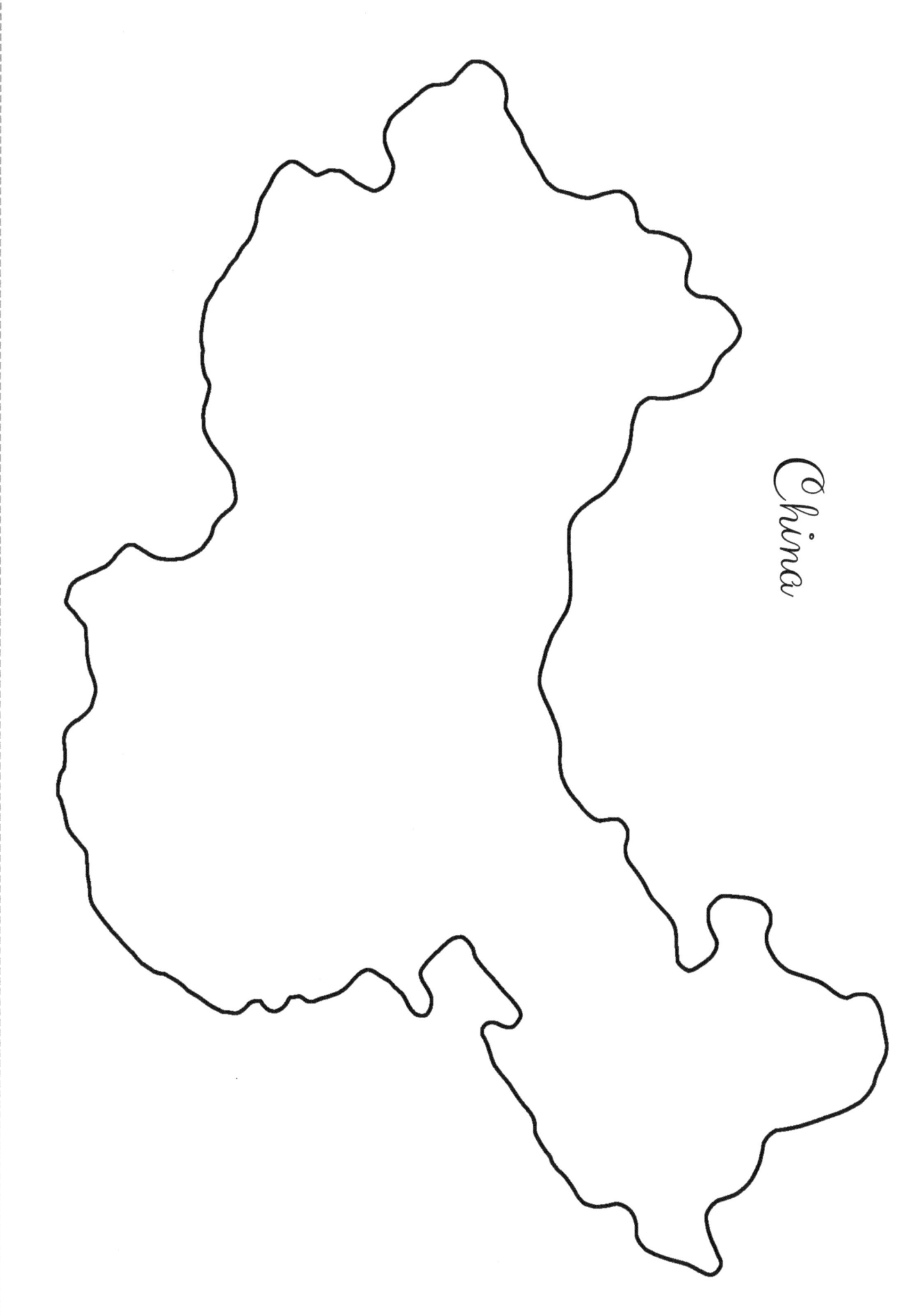

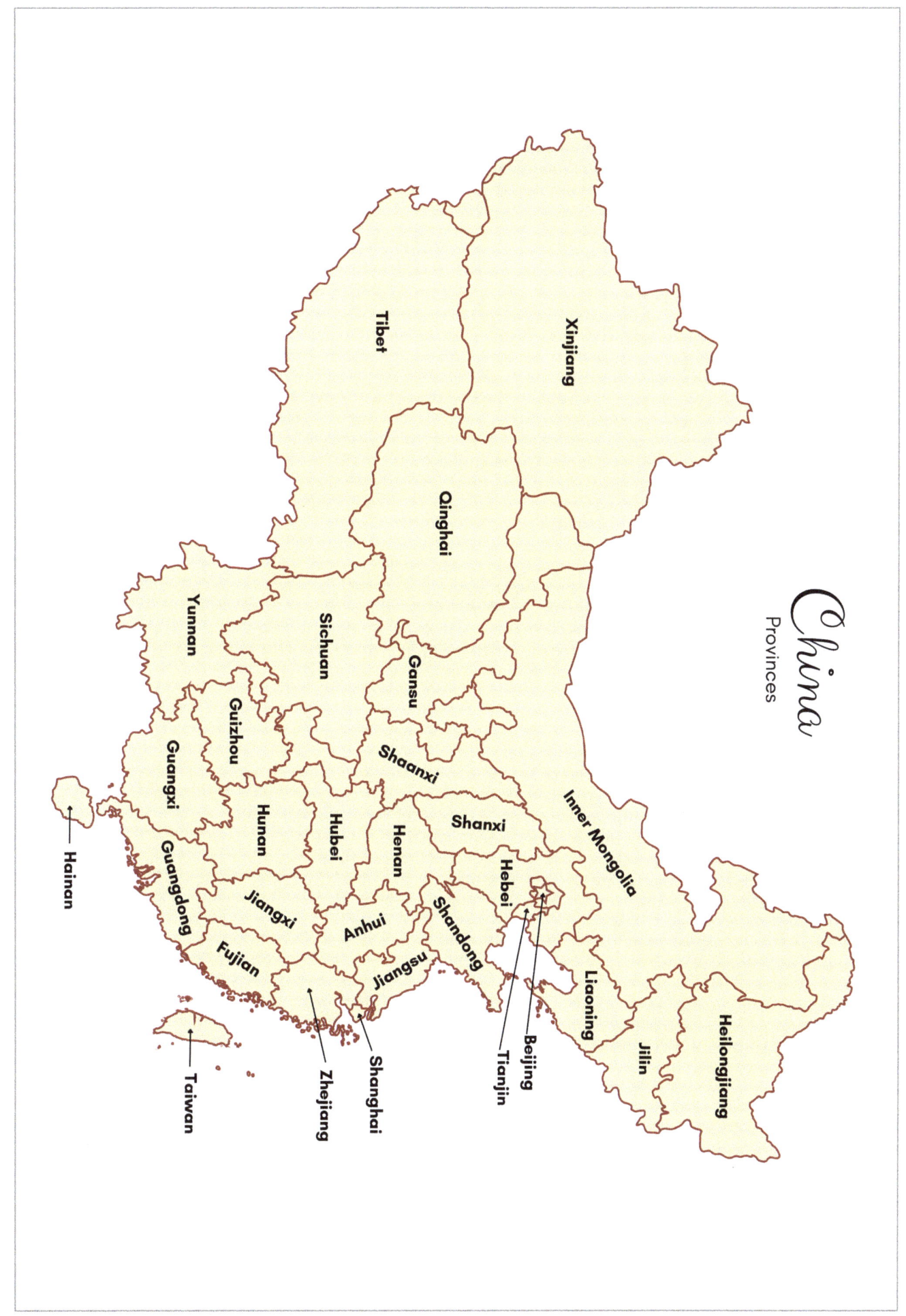

Asia Continent: China

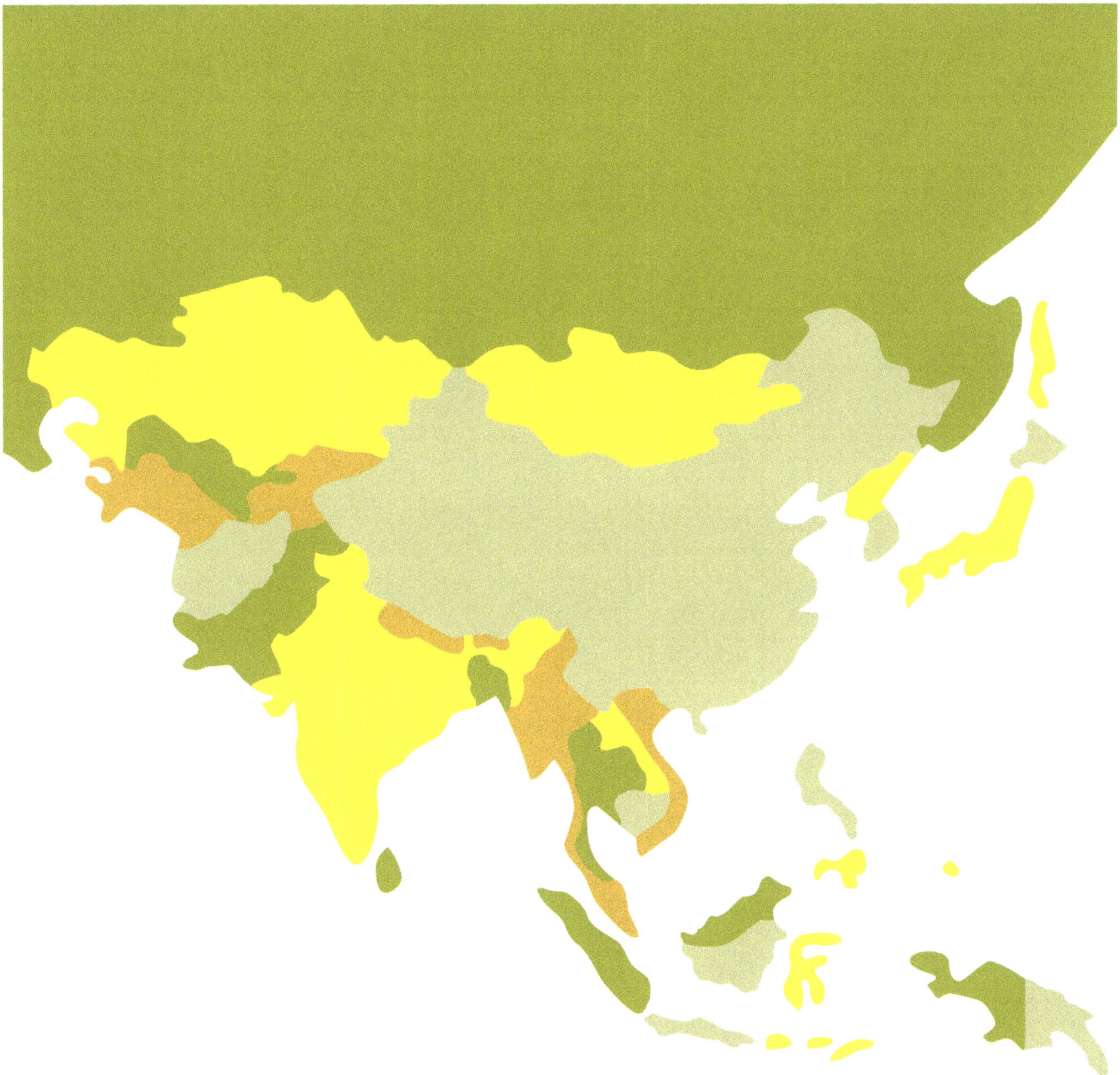

Cut out continent. Glue over corkboard or cardboard. Cut out flag and glue onto toothpick or straight pin. Mark country with flag.

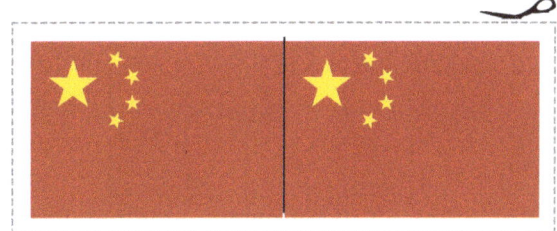

China Fun Facts

If you lined up every railroad track in China, it would circle the earth twice.

Despite being a very large country, China only has one time zone.

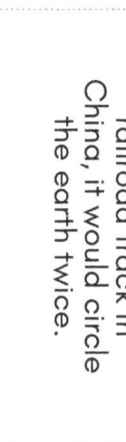

Fortune cookies aren't traditionally Chinese, they were invented in the USA.

The Forbidden City has over 9,000 rooms and is one of the largest/oldest imperial palaces in the world.

China's Bailong elevator is the world's heaviest and longest elevator. It carries people 300 meters up a cliff face.

China is the most populated country in the world, with over 1.4 billion people.

Chinese avoid using the number four because it is associated with death.

China builds new skyscrapers about every five days; they are the fastest growing country in the world.

China Fun Facts

Chinese brides wear red on their wedding day because red is a lucky color.

The Chinese invented ice cream about 4,000 years ago.

Chopsticks were originally used for cooking, not eating.

Every giant panda is owned by China. Pandas found around the world are only on loan.

China's Grand Canal is the world's oldest and longest canal at 1,114 miles (1,795 km). It has 24 locks and 60 bridges.

According to legend, tea was discovered by the Chinese emperor Shennong in 2737 B.C. when a tea leaf fell into his boiling water.

The mortar used to bind the stones of China's Great Wall was made with sticky rice!

China is the world's leading mushroom producer, including 60% of the world's mushroom varieties.

Chinese Timeline Period Cards

Xia Dynasty 夏
Yu the Great Illustration
2070 - 1600 BC

Shang Dynasty 商
Fu Hao Tomb
1600 - 1045 BC

Zhou Dynasty 周
Western Zhou Bronze Vessel
1046 - 256 BC

Qin Dynasty 秦
Tericotta Warriors
221 - 206 BC

Chinese Timeline Period Cards

Han Dynasty 漢

Silk Road Watchtower Ruins

202 BC - 220 AD

Three Kingdoms 三國時代

Biography of Bu Zhi from the Dunhuang manuscripts

220 - 280 AD

Jin Dynasty 晉

Lacquer screen, from the tomb of Sima Jinlong

266 - 420 AD

Sixteen Kingdoms of the Five Barbarians 十六國

Tongwancheng Ruins

304 - 439 AD

Chinese Timeline Period Cards

Sui Dynasty 隋

Yang Guang, Emperor of Sui
581 - 618 AD

Tang Dynasty 唐

Leshan Giant Buddha
618 - 907 AD

Five Dynasties & Ten Kingdoms 五代十國

Weiqi Players Painting
907 - 960 AD

Song Dynasty 宋

Liaodi Pagoda
960 - 1279 AD

Chinese Timeline Period Cards

Yuan Dynasty 元

Porcelain Dish
1271 - 1368 AD

Ming Dynasty 明

Great Wall
1368 - 1644 AD

Qing Dynasty 清

Medicine Book
1644 - 1912 AD

Republic of China 中華民國

Sun Yat-sen, first president of the Republic of China
1912 - 1949 AD

Chinese Timeline Period Cards

People's Republic of China
中华人民共和国
Beijing
1950 – Current

Chinese Zodiac Ring Cards

Calm, gentle, sympathetic — Goat

Animated, active, energetic — Horse

Lovely, honest, prudent — Dog

Observant, hardworking, courageous — Rooster

Chinese Zodiac Ring Cards

虎  Brave, competitive, unpredictable, confident — Tiger

蛇  Enigmatic, intelligent, wise — Snake

牛  Diligent, dependable, strong, determined — Ox

龙   Confident, intelligent, enthusiastic — Dragon

鼠  Quick-witted, resourceful, versatile, kind — Rat

兔  Quiet, elegant, kind, responsible — Rabbit

猴 Sharp, smart, curiosity — Monkey

豬  Compassionate, generous, diligent — Pig

Chinese Calendar Wheel

GREAT WALL OF CHINA MODEL

Instructions

The Great Wall of China is one of the most iconic landmarks in China. The majority of this structure was constructed during the Ming dynasty (1368–1644), with some sections built as early as the 7th century BC. The collective sections of the wall span over 21,000 kilometers (13,000 miles) and is considered one of the most impressive architectural feats in history!

Materials
- Great Wall of China Template
- Scissors
- Craft Glue
- Tape
- Craft Knife
- Clothespins (optional)

Cut out each piece of the Great Wall of China template. Locate tower 1, 2 & 3 pieces. Carefully fold along indicated lines. Using a craft knife, cut along wall insertion points carefully. Locate tower floor pieces. Using a craft knife, cut along indicated lines on tower 2 floor (the other towers do not have an extension). Carefully glue each floor into the top of the towers, working around the floor to create a square cylinder shape. The notched top of the tower should still be visible, with the floor positioned directly below the notching. Lastly, glue towers along sides, as indicated. Allow all

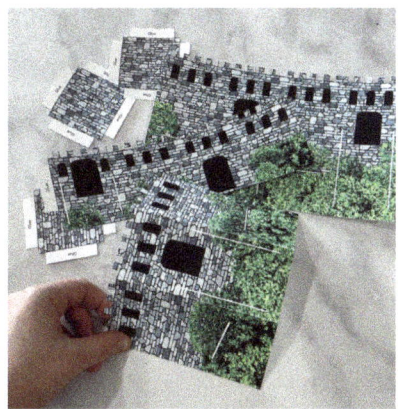

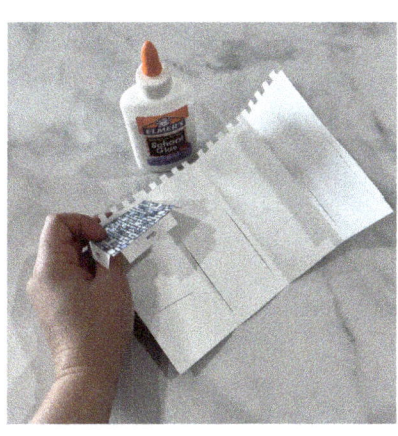

towers to dry completely. Locate the curved wall sides & floor. Glue tabs along floor to inside sides of both curved side pieces. The notched top of the wall should still be visible, with the floor positioned directly below the notching. *It may be helpful to use clothespins to hold pieces in place during the drying process if using craft glue.* Locate the sloped walls and floor. Again, glue tabs along floor piece to inside sides of both sloped-wall side pieces. The notched top of the wall should still be visible, with the floor positioned directly below notching. Set aside to dry. Lastly, locate the stair walls and floor. Fold floor piece along dashed lines, as indicated. Glue tabs along floor piece to inside sides of both stair-wall side pieces, with the angle of the "stairs" following the side angle of the walls, as indicated. On all wall sections, secure the bottom of each section with two stabilizer pieces, and glue into place. Allow to dry completely.

Insert stair-wall section into shorter insertion points on tower 3. Secure tabs inside tower with tape to secure into place. Insert curved-wall section into opposite side of tower, into insertion points on tower 3. Secure tabs inside tower with tape to secure into place. Locate tower 2 and insert onto far end of curved wall section. Again, secure in place inside tower with tape. Locate sloped wall section and secure into tower 2 the same way you have done with previous insertions. Lastly, insert tower 1 onto the shorter end of the sloped wall section and secure in place.

Locate tower 2 extension piece. Fold along dashed lines and glue into square shape, and glue into place with tab. Fold roof tabs inward and glue red roof piece onto top. Insert into slits on tower 2 floor. Locate interior grass pieces 1, 2 & 3. Cut along one side of notches, as illustrated. Glue notches inward so it creates a sloped surface. Allow to dry completely. Glue interior grass 2 & 3 together along tab, as indicated.

Insert tab on interior grass 1 piece into tower 3 insertion point. Secure inside tower with tape. Insert tab on combined interior grass 2 & 3 pieces into tower 2 and tower 1 as illustrated. Secure inside tower with tape. Glue remaining tabs alone inside edge of interior grass sections with glue along sides of walls. Position paper so that the outside edge of interior grass section is flush with the bottom of the diorama. Glue interior grass 1 to combined interior grass 2 & 3 along tab and allow to dry completely. Locate exterior grass pieces 1, 2 & 3. Cut along one side of notches, as illustrated. Glue notches inward so it creates a sloped surface. Allow to dry.

Glue exterior grass pieces 1 & 2 together along side tabs, as indicated. Repeat with sides of 2 & 3 to form a long curved surface. Insert exterior grass piece 1 into tower 2 as indicated. Repeat with tab on exterior grass piece 3 into tower 1. Secure inside towers with tape. Glue remaining tabs along inside edge of exterior grass sections to the sides of the walls. Position paper so that the outside edge of exterior grass sections are flush with the bottom of the diorama. Allow to dry completely.

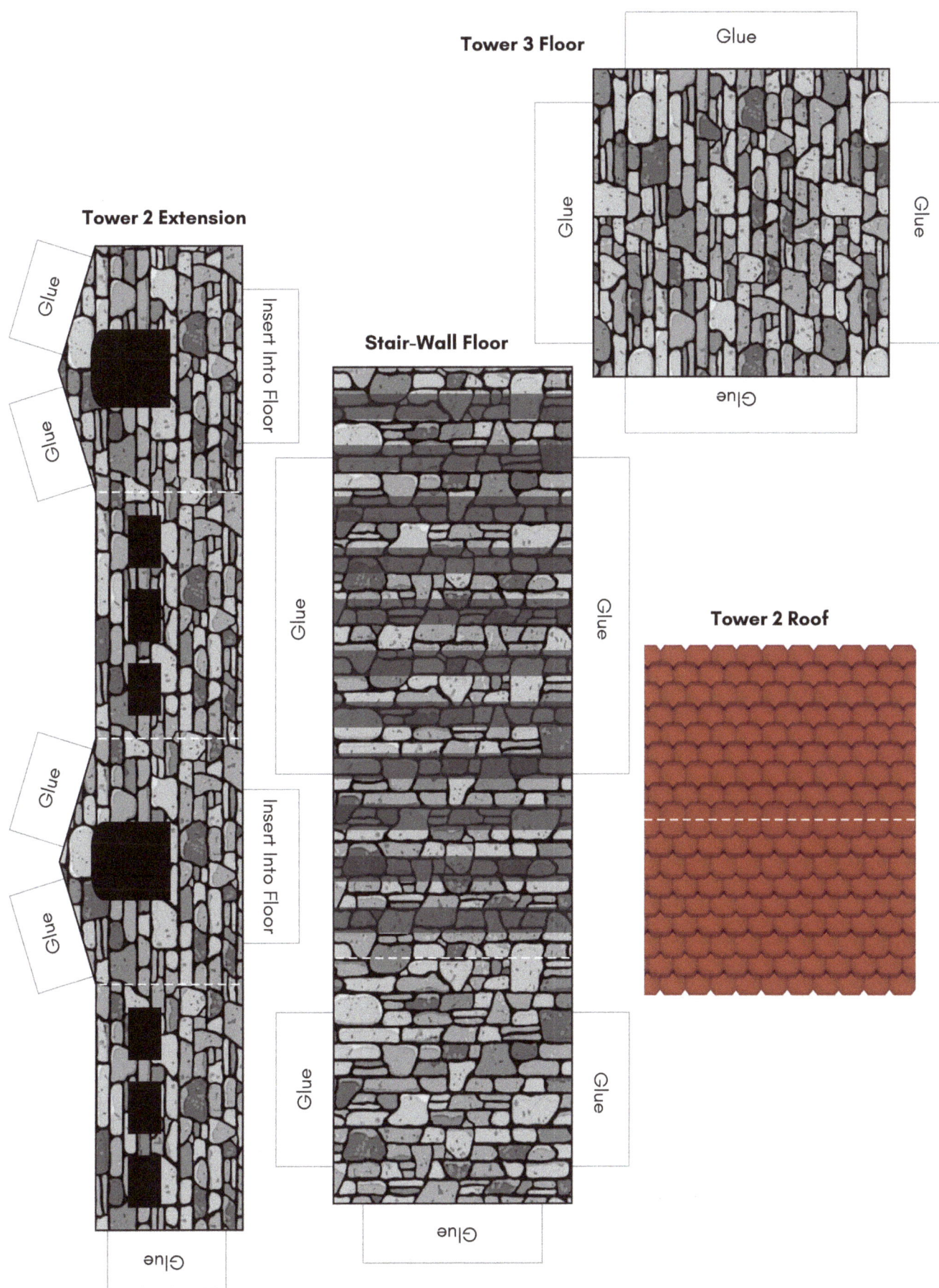

Glue

Tower 3

Tower 2

Glue

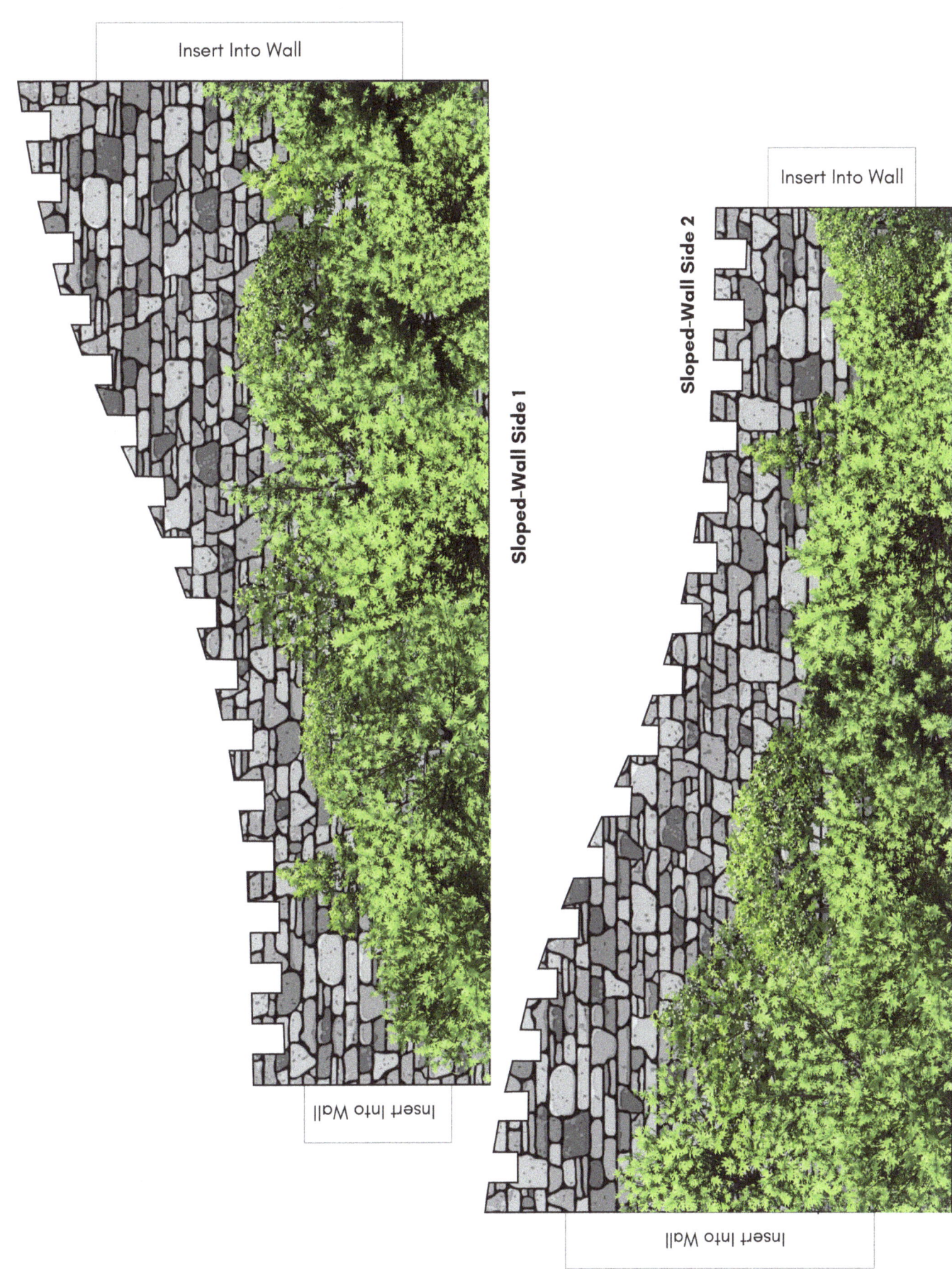

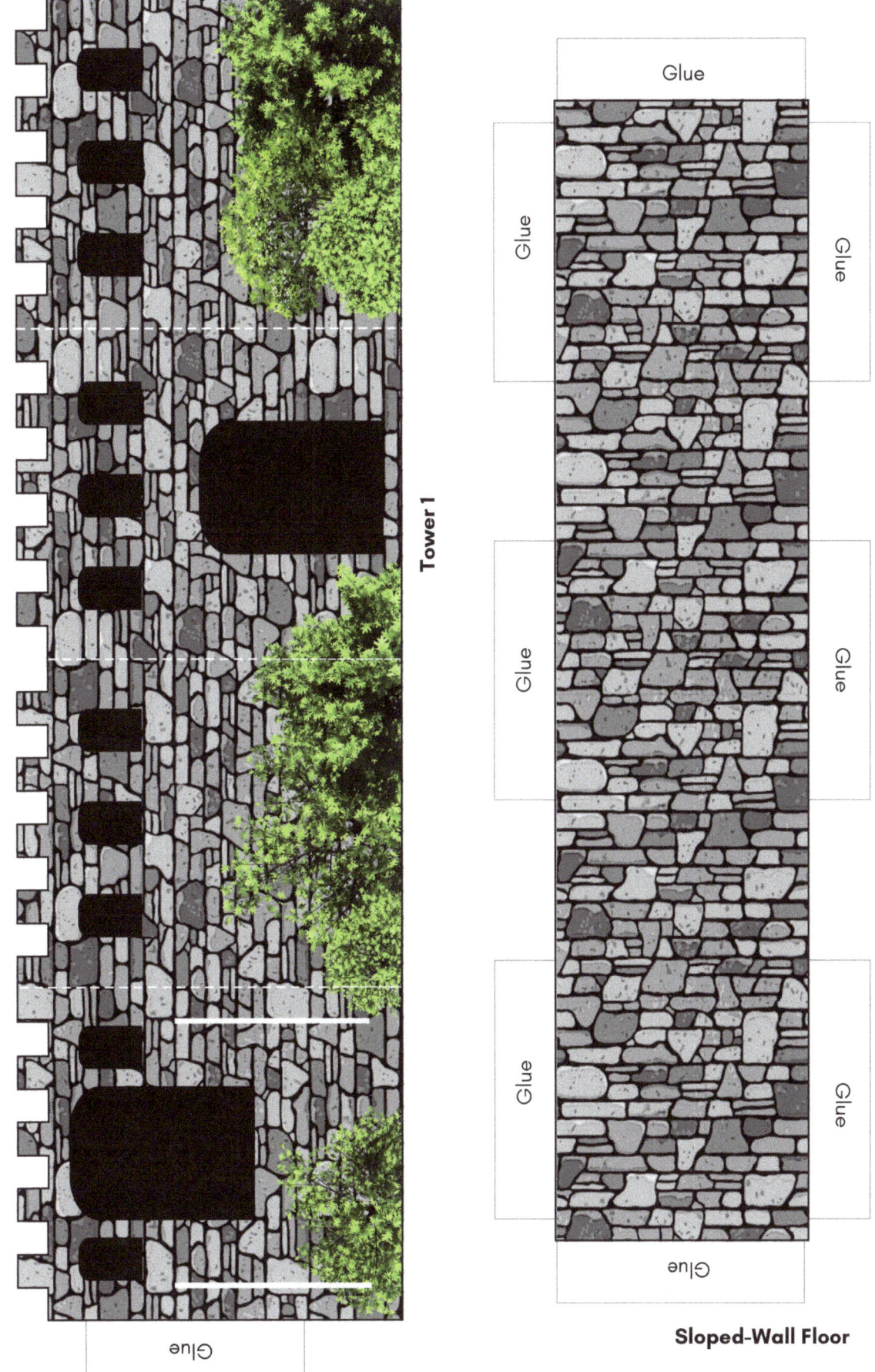

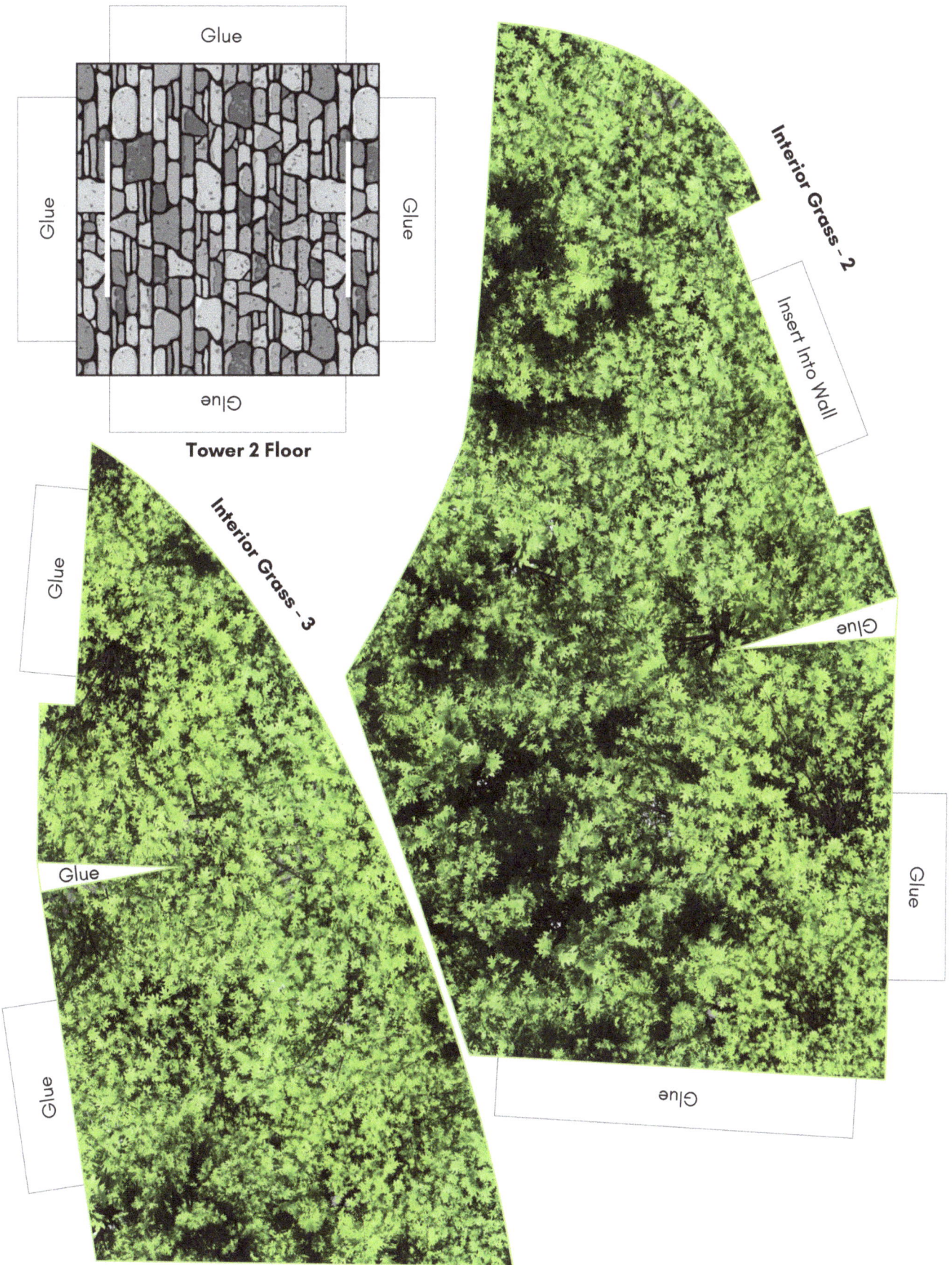

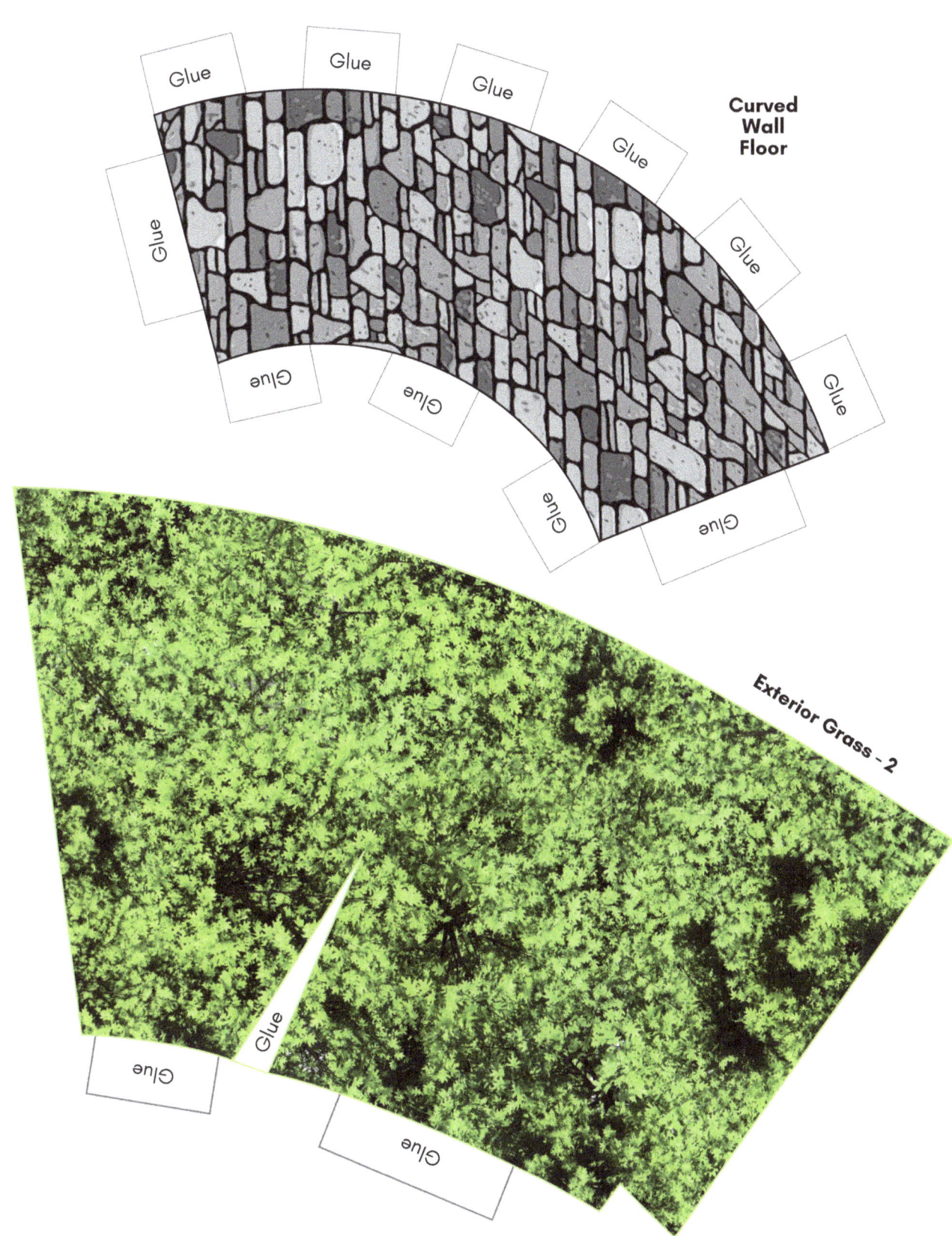

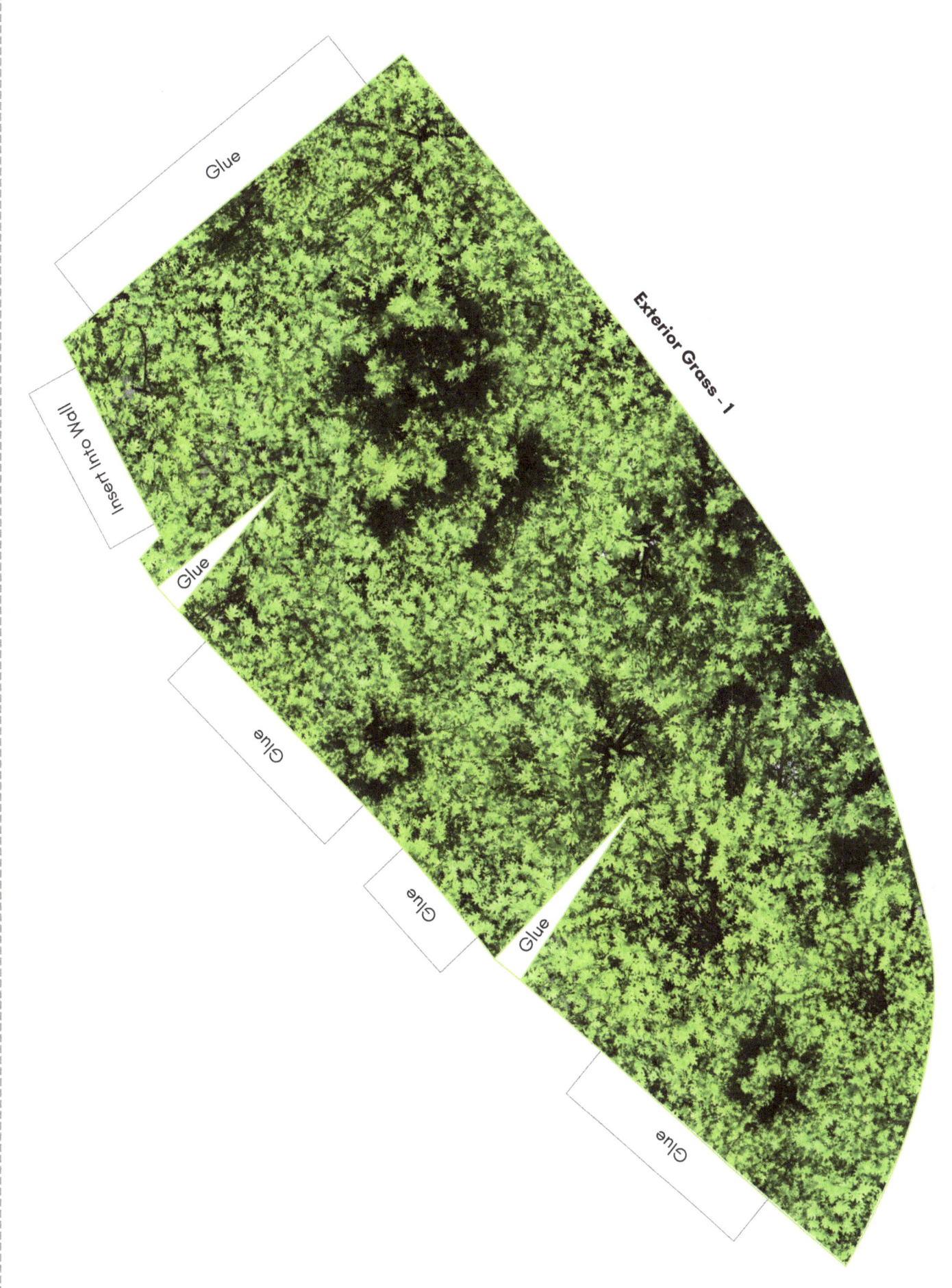

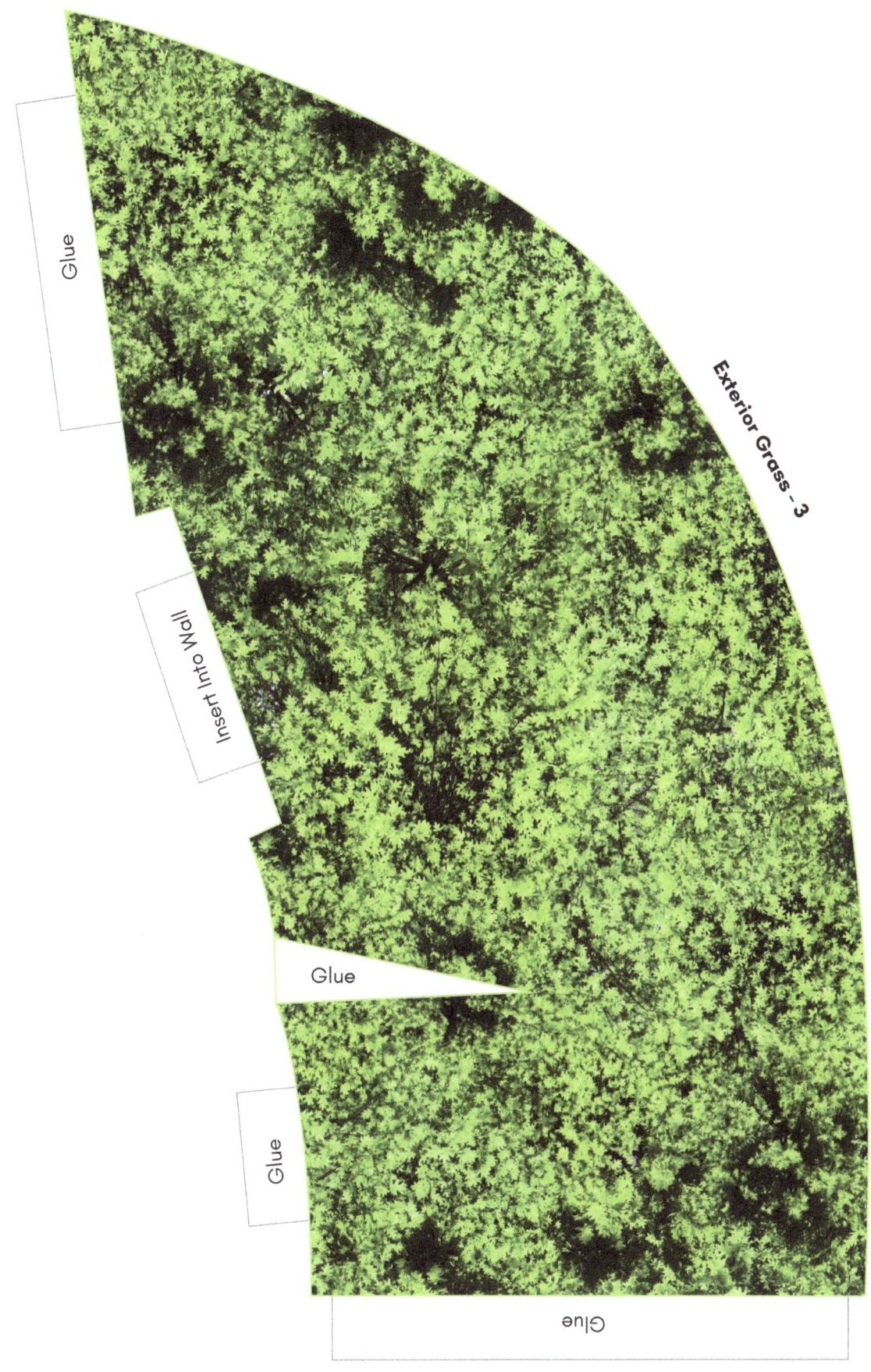

CLOTHESPIN DRAGON

Materials
- Dragon Template
- Crayons/Markers
- Scissors
- Craft/Hot Glue
- Clothespins

Instructions

The Chinese dragon (also known as Long or Lung), is a central legendary creature in Chinese mythology, folklore, and culture. This activity allows children to work on coloring and scissor skills as well as create a fun movable dragon head.

Provide the child with the dragon template. Allow the child to color the dragon outline, if desired. Crayons or markers can be used. Cut out each dragon outline - it may be necessary to have an adult assist with this step. Cut dragon in half along dotted lines. Using craft or hot glue (adult supervision required), Glue top of paper dragon head onto top of a clothespin. Repeat on bottom with the bottom piece of paper dragon head. Allow glue to thoroughly dry before using.

Open the clothespin and the dragon will "open" it's mouth.

Clothespin Dragon

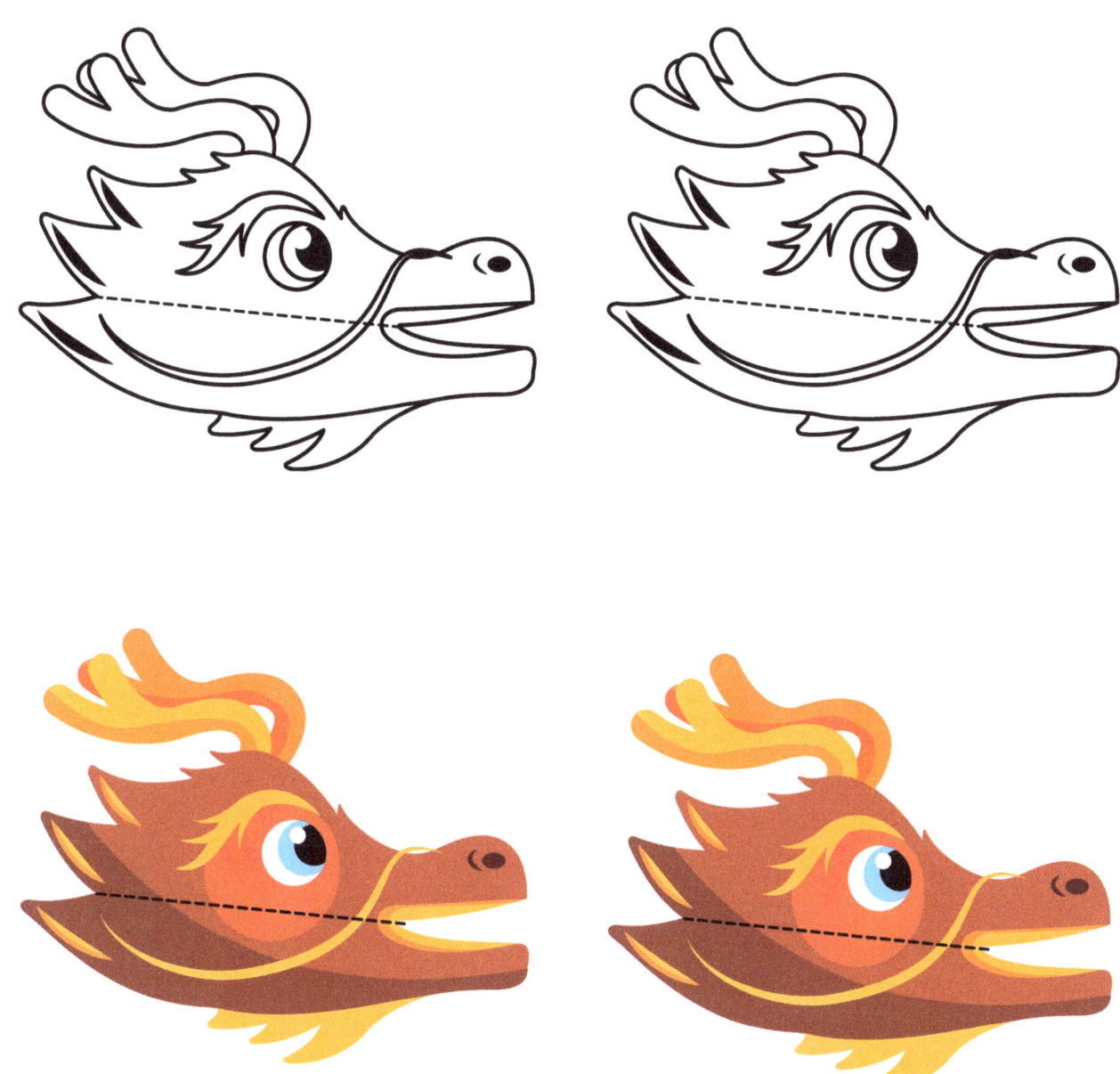

China Fauna (3-Part Cards)

Giant Panda

Yak

Chow Chow

Palla's Cat

China Fauna (3-Part Cards)

Giant Panda

Yak

Chow Chow

Palla's Cat

China Fauna (3-Part Cards)

Snub Nosed Monkey

Baiji

Pheasant

Tiger

China Fauna (3-Part Cards)

Snub Nosed Monkey

Baiji

Pheasant

Tiger

Life Cycle Spinner

Life Cycle of the *Panda*

ears | head
eyes | nose
mouth | paw

| back | leg | tail | belly |

PANDA COUNTING

Instructions

Pandas are iconic indigenous animals of China. One of the main parts of their diet is bamboo and this fun activity allows children to work on numbers 1-20 and recognize them in line format.

Provide the printed panda illustration, number circles and bamboo stick templates. Laminate for additional durability, if desired. Cut each piece out. Younger children may need assistance with this step. Place a number on the panda. Have the child count out appropriate number of bamboo sticks to correspond with that number. For younger children, start with numbers 1-10, increase number as they master the smaller numbers. Show the child a certain amount of bamboo sticks and have them find the corresponding numeral.

Materials
- Panda, Numbers & Bamboo Templates
- Laminator (optional)
- Scissors

Panda Counting

Panda Counting

1	2	3	4
5	6	7	8
9	10	11	12
13	14	15	16
17	18	19	20

Panda Counting

Tiger Mask

Cut out mask. Cut out eye shapes and glue onto craft stick or punch holes on side and use elastic string to hold on face.

Panda Mask

Cut out mask. Cut out eye shapes and glue onto craft stick or punch holes on side and use elastic string to hold on face.

THE STORY OF THE CHINESE ZODIAC

When it came time to leave, the Cat was sleeping. The Rat realized he would have to be cunning in order to win, so he left his friend sleeping. This is why cats and rats have hated each other ever since.

 The Dog was one of the best swimmers, but he came in next because he had stopped to take a bath.

The Pig was last because he had fallen asleep.

Once upon a time, the Jade Emperor (who ruled China), decided to name each year after an animal, to help people keep track of time. He sent a message to the animals to have them meet him near a river.

1

Since this time, the years have been counted by each of these twelve animals.

THE END.

10

After the animals were all assembled, the Jade Emperor told them that they would have a swimming race to determine who would be named first.

The Rat found the Ox, the largest, strongest animal, and asked if he could ride on his head.

3

The Goat, Monkey & Rooster worked together by making a raft and all safely crossed;

...the Emperor was pleased with their teamwork.

8

The Dragon finished next, only behind the others because he had helped the other animals.

The Horse and Snake followed; the Snake scared the Horse and managed to sneak ahead.

7

The Ox agreed, and the two set off across the river.

4

Assembly Instructions

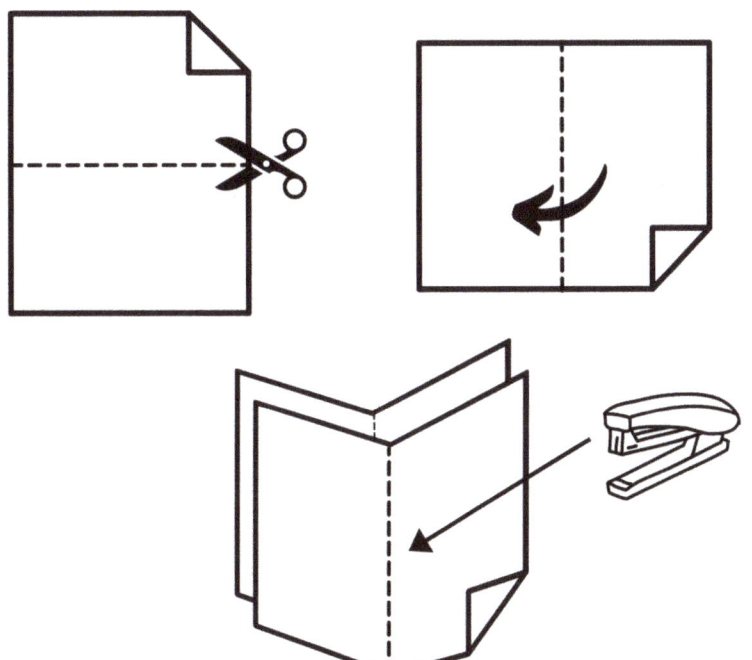

Cut paper in half on lines. Fold each page of book as indicated. Collate together so pages match up appropriately. Staple spine to hold together.

The Rat crossed the river safely on the Ox's back, but just before they reached the other side, the Rat jumped onto land, and reached the side first.

Next came the Tiger,

followed by the Rabbit who had hopped across on stones.

Chinese Traditional Clothing

Chinese Traditional Clothing

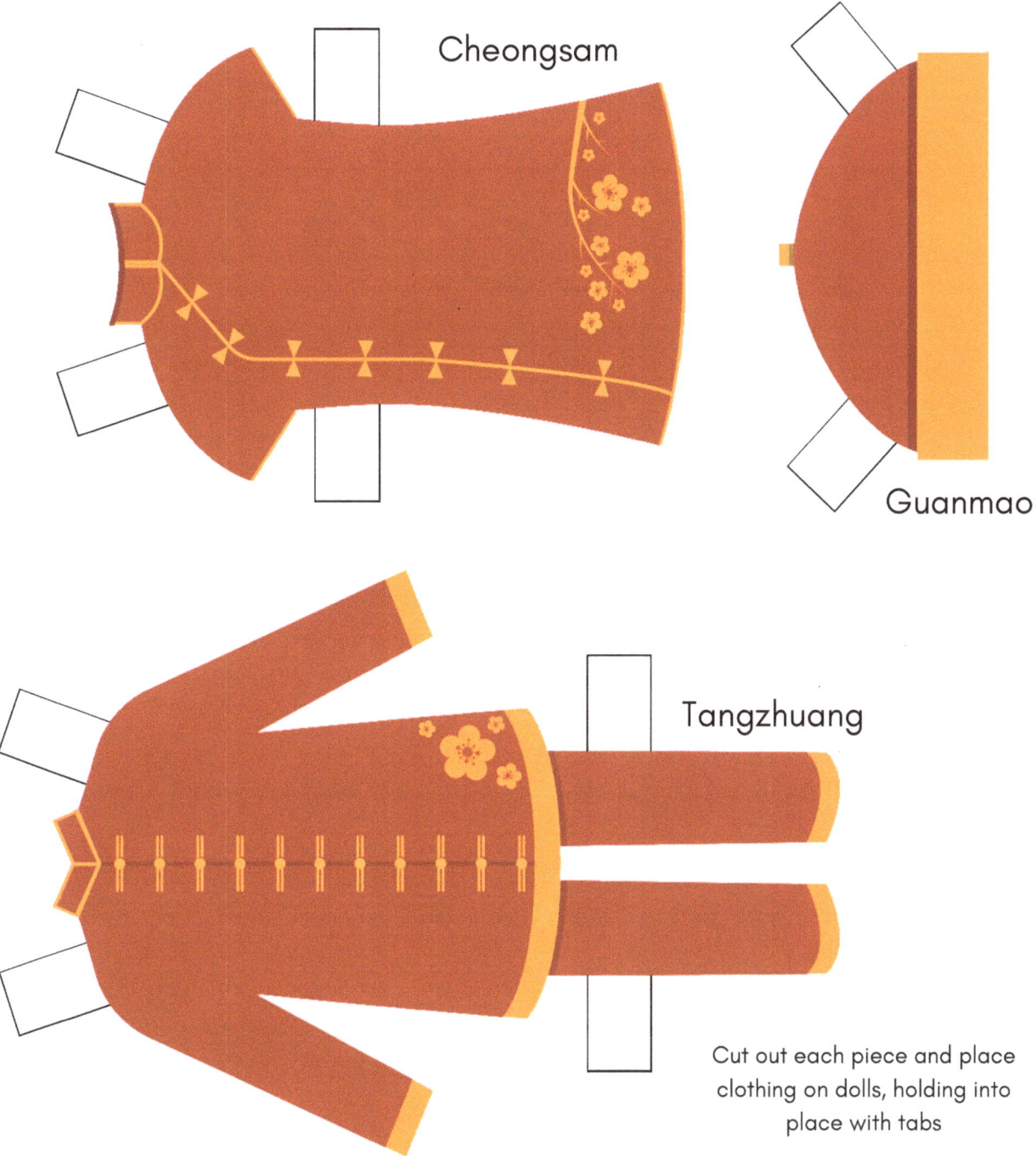

Cheongsam

Guanmao

Tangzhuang

Cut out each piece and place clothing on dolls, holding into place with tabs

LUNAR NEW YEAR SLIME

Instructions

Slime is created when activators such as borax, borax-based saline solution, or liquid starch change the position of the molecules in the glue in a process called cross-linking This fun activity demonstrates this change and provides a fun sensory-filled slime that is Chinese New Year themed.

Materials
- PVA based glue (clear or red)
- Borax/Borax Contact Solution
- Red Food Coloring (optional)
- Mixing Bowl & Spoon
- Baking Soda
- Gold Sequins

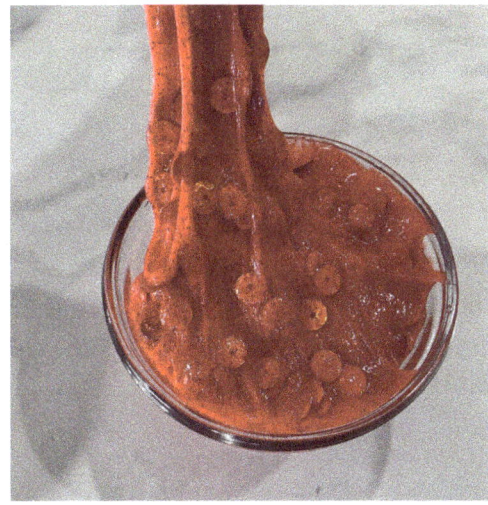

Pour eight ounces of PVA based glue into mixing bowl. If glue is not already colored, add red food coloring. Mix in two teaspoons baking soda. Add fine glitter if desired for added sparkle. Pour two tablespoons of borax or borax based contact solution into bowl. Mixture will start becoming thicker. Add gold sequins and continue to mix by hand until slime starts to become less sticky and form a stretchy glob.

Enjoy!

LUNAR NEW YEAR SENSORY TRAY

Materials
- Red Scatter/Vase Filler
- Red Pom Pons
- Gold Scatter/Vase Filler
- Gold Coins & Bells
- Red/Yellow Caps
- Bamboo Sticks

Instructions

Lunar New Year is one of the most important holidays in China, celebrated between late January and early February. The festival was traditionally a time to honor deities and ancestors. Red is a lucky color in China, and decorations for the New Year celebrations include both red and gold colors, specifically related to money as red envelopes containing money are popular gifts. Arrange red acrylic vase filler, pom-poms or assorted red items. Add gold beads and gold coins. Get creative with gold or yellow caps. Add bamboo sticks and gold bells for additional sensory experiences. Allow child to arrange/sort and feel the objects. Adult supervision is required for younger children due to small size of items.

Red Envelope

Cut out the *Red Envelope*. Fold in half along indicate line. Using tape of glue stick, connect outside edge together on short and long side, leaving the opposite short side with flap free. Place money in the envelope and fold flap down to "close" envelope. Give it as a gift during lunar new year.

RIBBON DANCING

Materials
- 1/2" (or wider) craft stick
- 1 Yard of Ribbon
- Hot glue Gun (or craft glue, allowing adequate drying time)

Instructions

The Chinese Ribbon Dance is a traditional dance that has been performed for more than a 1000 years. The Chinese legend has it that Emperor Tang who ruled China from 713-755 AD had a dream that he was in the moon palace with many fairies singing and dancing who were wearing beautiful multicolored long robes.

Glue one yard of ribbon onto a 1/2" craft stick. Glue in several places so the ribbon is securely on the stick. Have the child wave the ribbon around creating designs in the air or floor. Circles overhead, circles in the front of the body, circles on the side of the body, Snakes horizontal or vertical in front or on the side of the body (small curvy movements), Turns, Letters of the name, and Figure eights both vertical and horizontal.

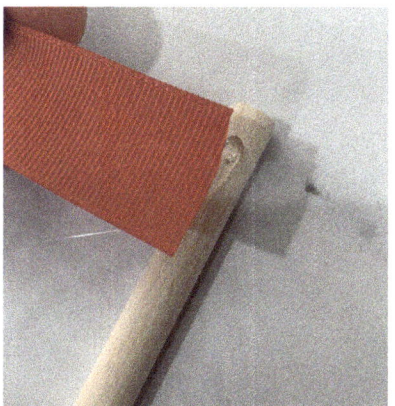
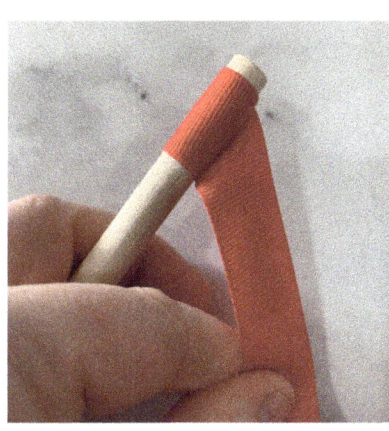
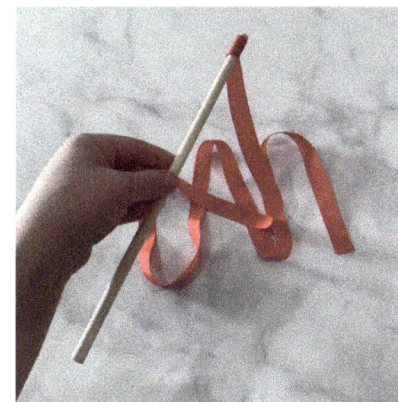

VEGETABLE CHOW MEIN

ingredients

- 7 ounces egg noodles
- 1 carrot, shredded
- 1 cup snow peas
- 2 tablespoons spring onions, chopped
- 1/2 cup bean sprouts
- 1/2 cup cabbage, shredded
- 1/4 cup green pepper, sliced
- 1/4 cup broccoli flowerets
- 1/4 cup mushrooms, sliced
- 2 teaspoons oil
- 1 garlic clove, crushed
- 1 Tablespoon soy sauce
- 2 teaspoons honey
- 1 teaspoon ketchup
- 1 teaspoon lemon juice

directions

- Boil noodles according to directions until soft, drain.
- Prepare vegetables into shredded, sliced or bite sized pieces as indicated.
- Stir-fry oil and garlic in wok (or pan) for 30 seconds, then add noodles and vegetables.
- Mix together soy, honey, ketchup and lemon juice in a small bowl and add to noodles and vegetables.
- Stir fry until vegetables are cooked, but still slightly crunchy. Serve hot.

Vegetable Chow Mein

INGREDIENTS

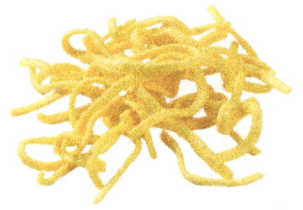
EGG NOODLES

CARROT

SNOW PEAS

SCALLIONS

BEAN SPROUTS

CABBAGE

GREEN PEPPER

BROCCOLI

MUSHROOMS

OIL

GARLIC

SOY SAUCE

HONEY

KETCHUP

LEMON JUICE

PAPER MAKING

Instructions

The Chinese invented papermaking approximately two thousand years ago, in AD 105 during the Eastern Han Dynasty. Paper is created from processing cellulose fibers from wood, rags, grasses or other vegetable sources. For this activity, scrap paper is more than adequate (completed workbooks, extras, etc).

Materials
- Scrap Paper
- Hot Water
- Mixing Bowl
- Blender
- Strainer
- Wax Paper
- Cooking Sheet

Tear into small pieces and pour boiling water onto paper and allow to soak for 15-20 minutes. Blend in blender or food processor until smooth, adding more water if necessary. Strain water through mesh and flatten onto cooking sheet. Use wax paper to avoid paper sticking to sheet and flatten with roller (or hands). Remove top layer to allow to dry.

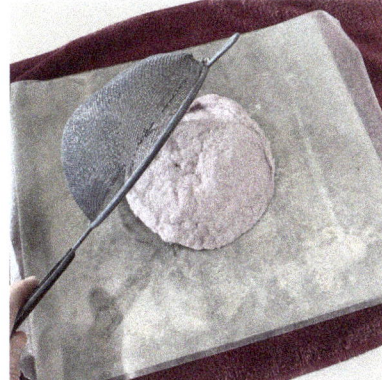

PAPER LANTERNS

Instructions

Paper lanterns have been used for centuries as decoration and part of festivals throughout Asia. These paper lanterns are an important part of the Chinese New Year celebrations.

Choose a lantern template. Cut off the edges of the lantern. Fold lantern in half and cut along printed lines. Cut small notches, as indicated, on the top and bottom, and slide these together to hold lantern sides in place. Tape or glue into place. Punch two small holes in the top of the lantern to fit a pipe cleaner or tie a string to use as a handle.

Optional: Use lantern template as a pattern and create additional lanterns in other colors from construction paper. Children can decorate it with crayons or markers prior to assembly, and add stickers or embellishments after it is assembled.

Materials

- Colored Paper Lantern Templates
- Colored Construction Paper
- Scissors & Hole Punch
- Tape (or craft glue)
- Pipe Cleaners/String

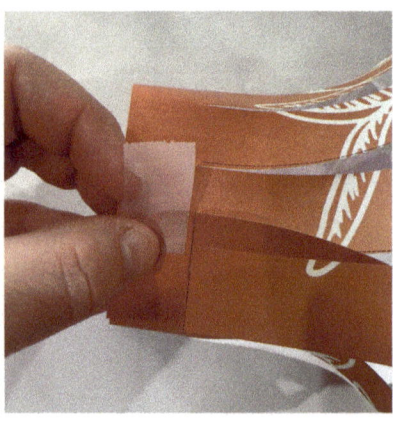
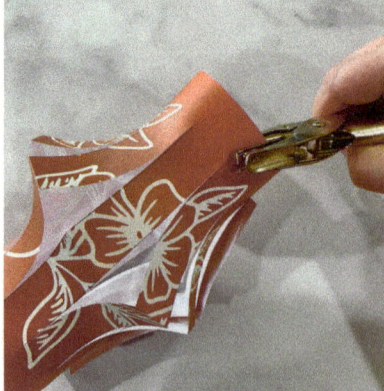

FRYING PAN GONG

Instructions

The invention of the gong has been attributed to the Chinese around 500 AD. Today, the Chinese continue to use gongs for many ceremonial functions, including announcing important political and religious figures and gathering men together for battle.

Materials
- Metal Pots/Pans
- Large Utensil

Provide child a metal pan. Hold by handle and allow them to tap the center of the back of the pan with a large utensil (metal works best, such as a spoon) to create noise. Have the child tap once and allow sounds to reverberate before hitting again. Experiment with different size pans.

Discuss: How do the sounds vary - are they low or high pitch? How long do they last? Try with different sized pots and pans. Does the sound change? If so, how? Do different utensils affect the sound?

Chinese Currency

人民币 *Renminbi "People's Currency"*

The Yuan is the main unit of the Chinese Renminbi currency. The Jiao is a subdivision worth 1/10 of a Yuan and the Fen is a second subdivision, worth 1/100 of a Yuan.

*This is a sample of some of the currency in circulation. Please note that some of the money depicted may be larger or smaller in reality and these pages only include one side in order to adhere to legal requirements regarding currency reproduction for educational and artistic use.

Chinese Currency

人民币 Renminbi "People's Currency"

The Yuan is the main unit of the Chinese Renminbi currency. The Jiao is a subdivision worth 1/10 of a Yuan and the Fen is a second subdivision, worth 1/100 of a Yuan.

Ancient Coin

*This is a sample of some of the currency in circulation. Please note that some of the money depicted may be larger or smaller in reality and these pages only include one side in order to adhere to legal requirements regarding currency reproduction for educational and artistic use.

Chinese Currency

人民币 *Renminbi "People's Currency"*

The Yuan is the main unit of the Chinese Renminbi currency. The Jiao is a subdivision worth 1/10 of a Yuan and the Fen is a second subdivision, worth 1/100 of a Yuan.

*This is a sample of some of the currency in circulation. Please note that some of the money depicted may be larger or smaller in reality and these pages only include one side in order to adhere to legal requirements regarding currency reproduction for educational and artistic use.

Units of Measurement - Mountains

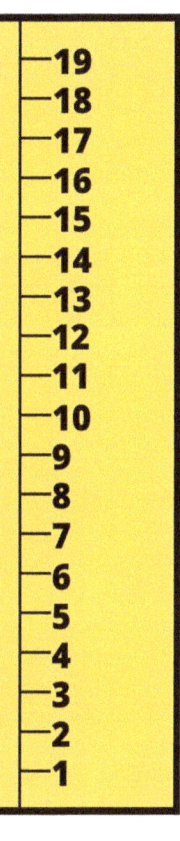

The tallest mountain in the world is Mount Everest, located in the Himalayan mountain range along the China-Nepal border. Measuring a total height of 8,848.86 m (29,032 ft) this peak was first officially summitted in 1953 by Edmund Hillary and Tenzing Norgay.

Use the included ruler to measure the height of mountain peaks throughout the world. Identify how many units of measurement each is. Compare to the other mountains. Which is the tallest? Which is the shortest? Put them in order of height. Which mountains surprise you with their height?

Units of Measurement - Mountains

Units of Measurement - Mountains

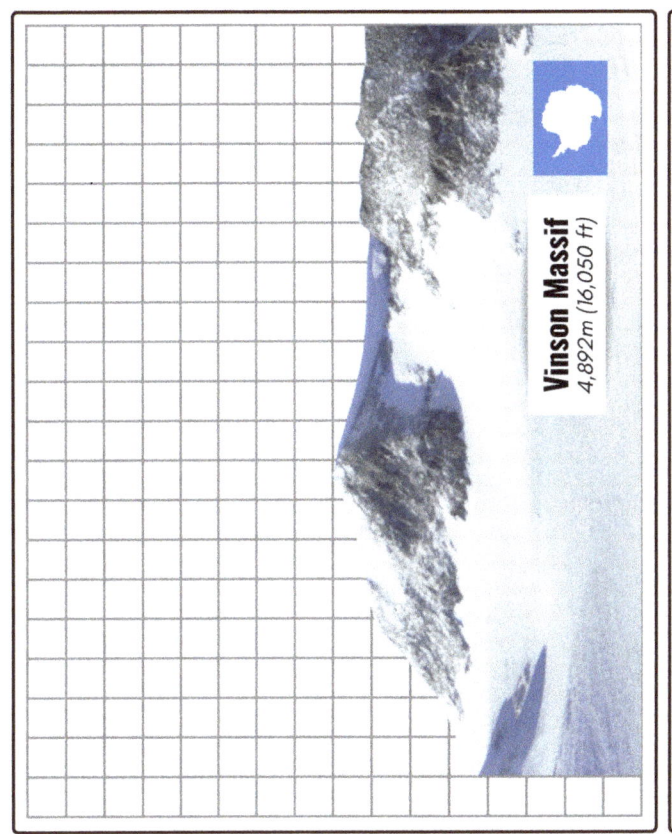

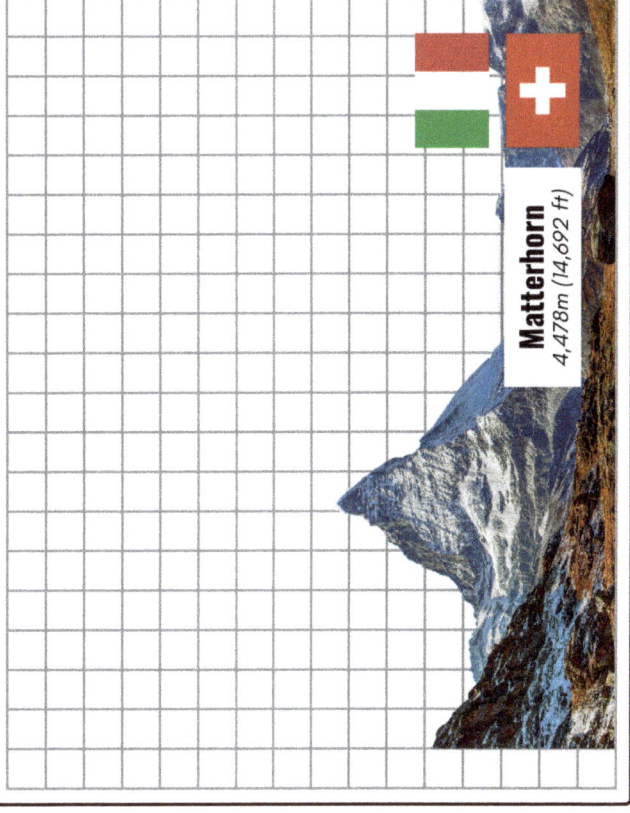

Units of Measurement - Mountains

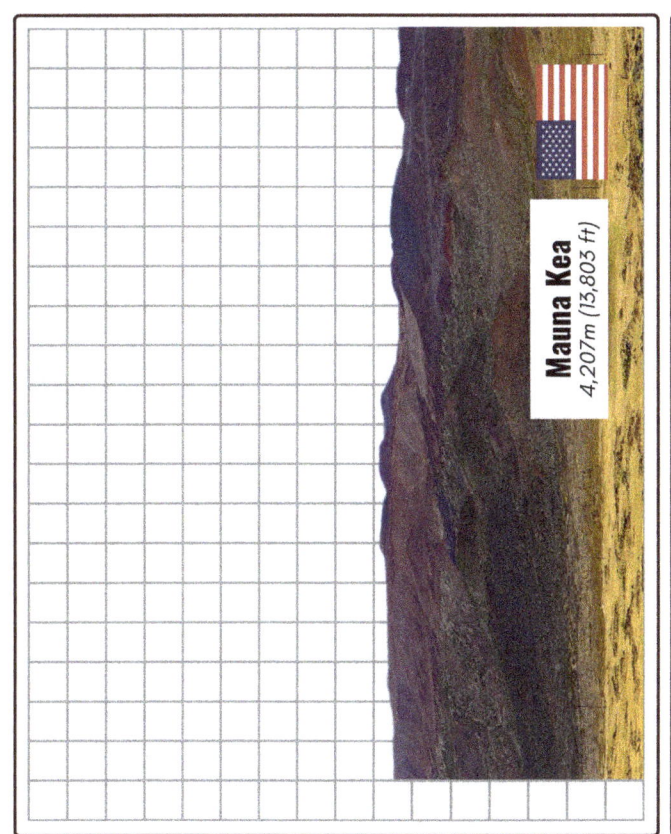
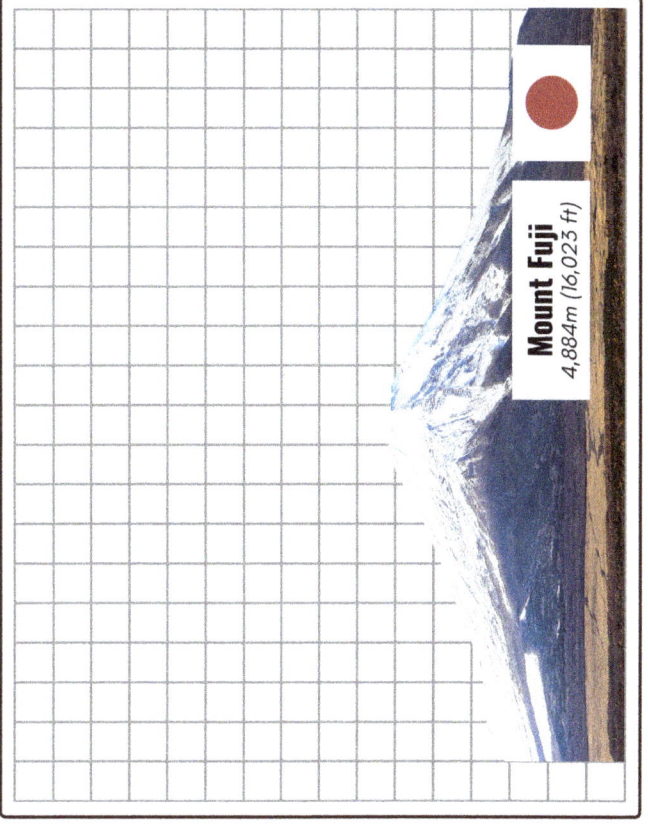

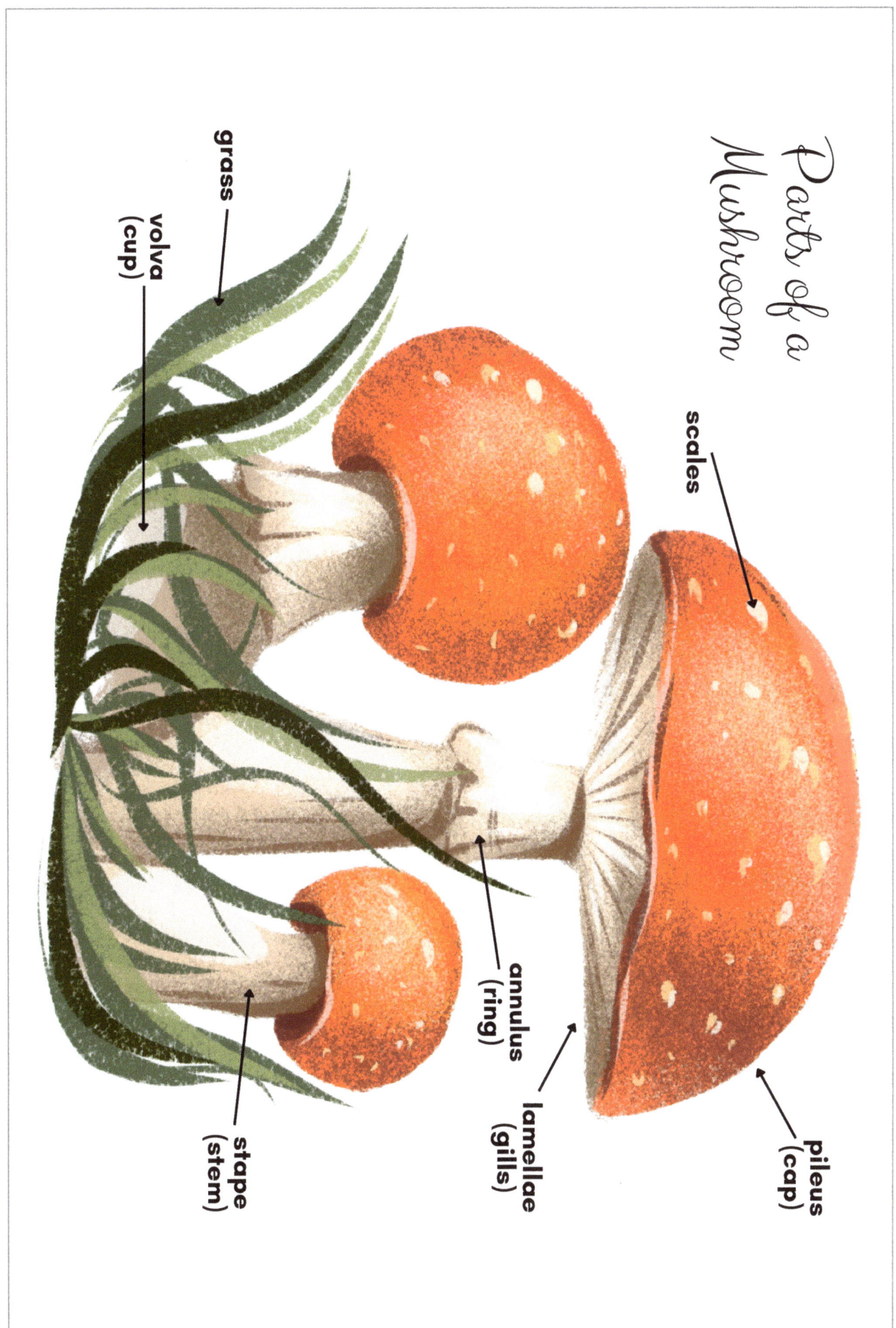

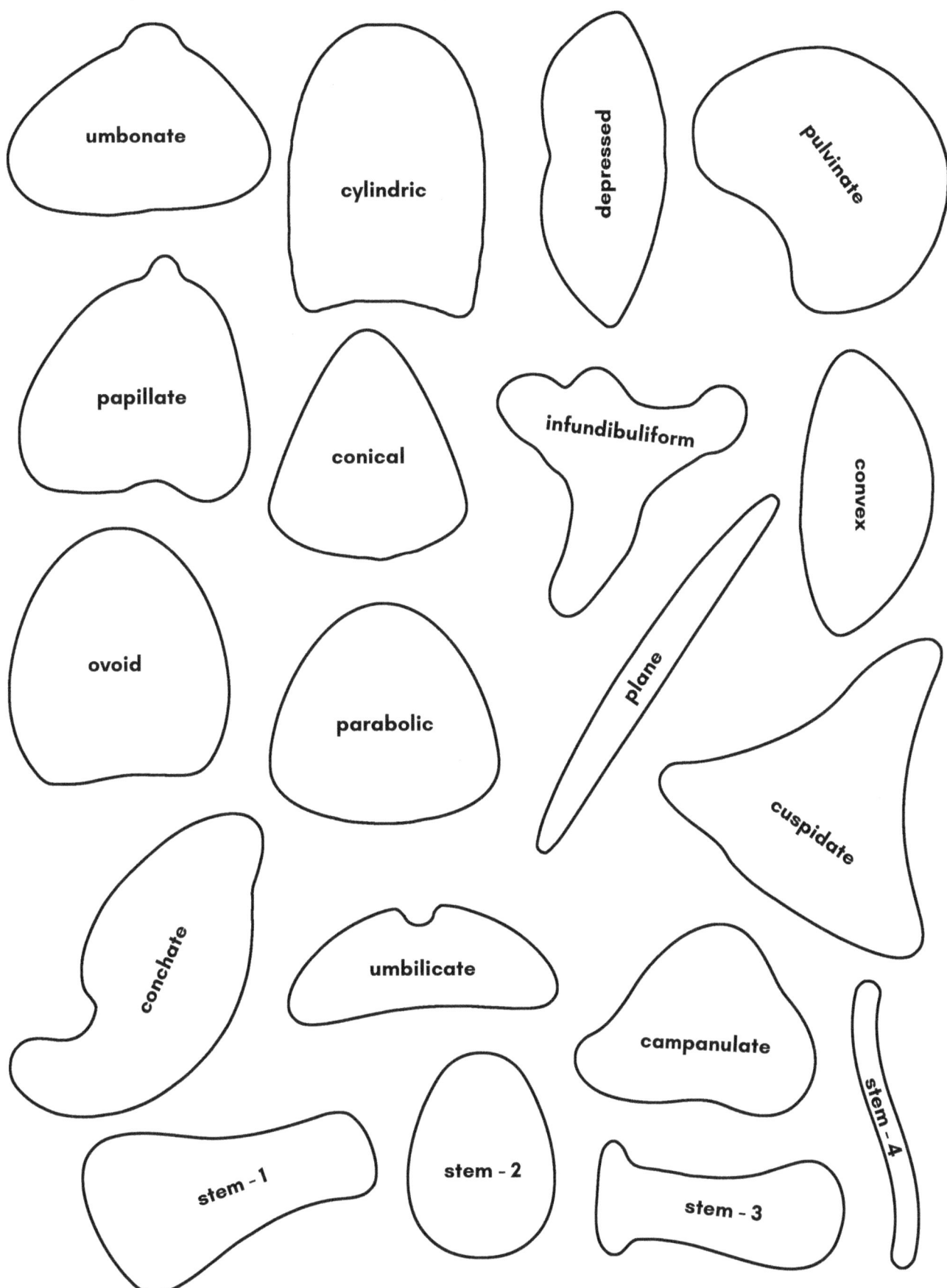

Mushroom Pileus Shape Cards

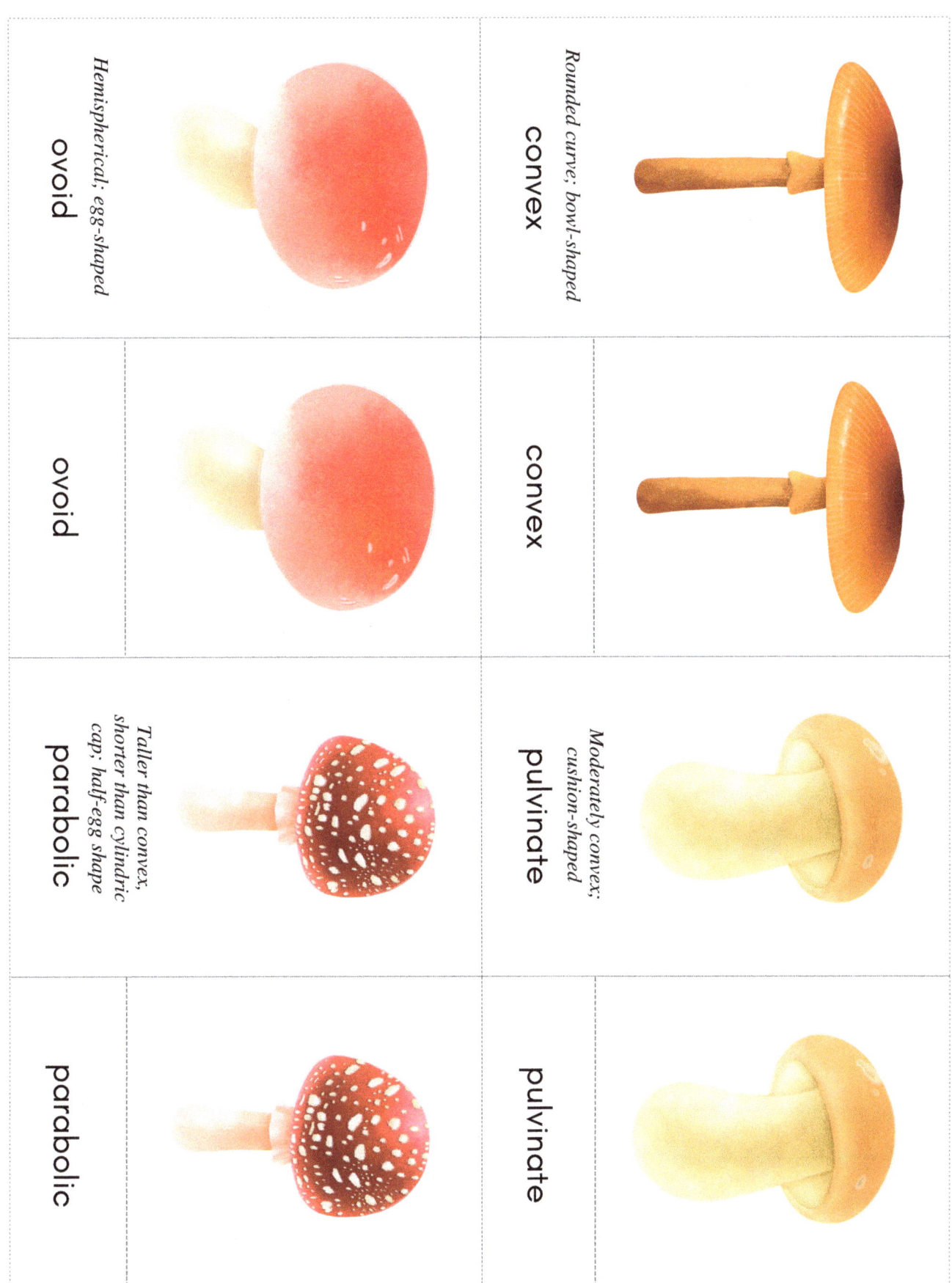

Mushroom Pileus Shape Cards

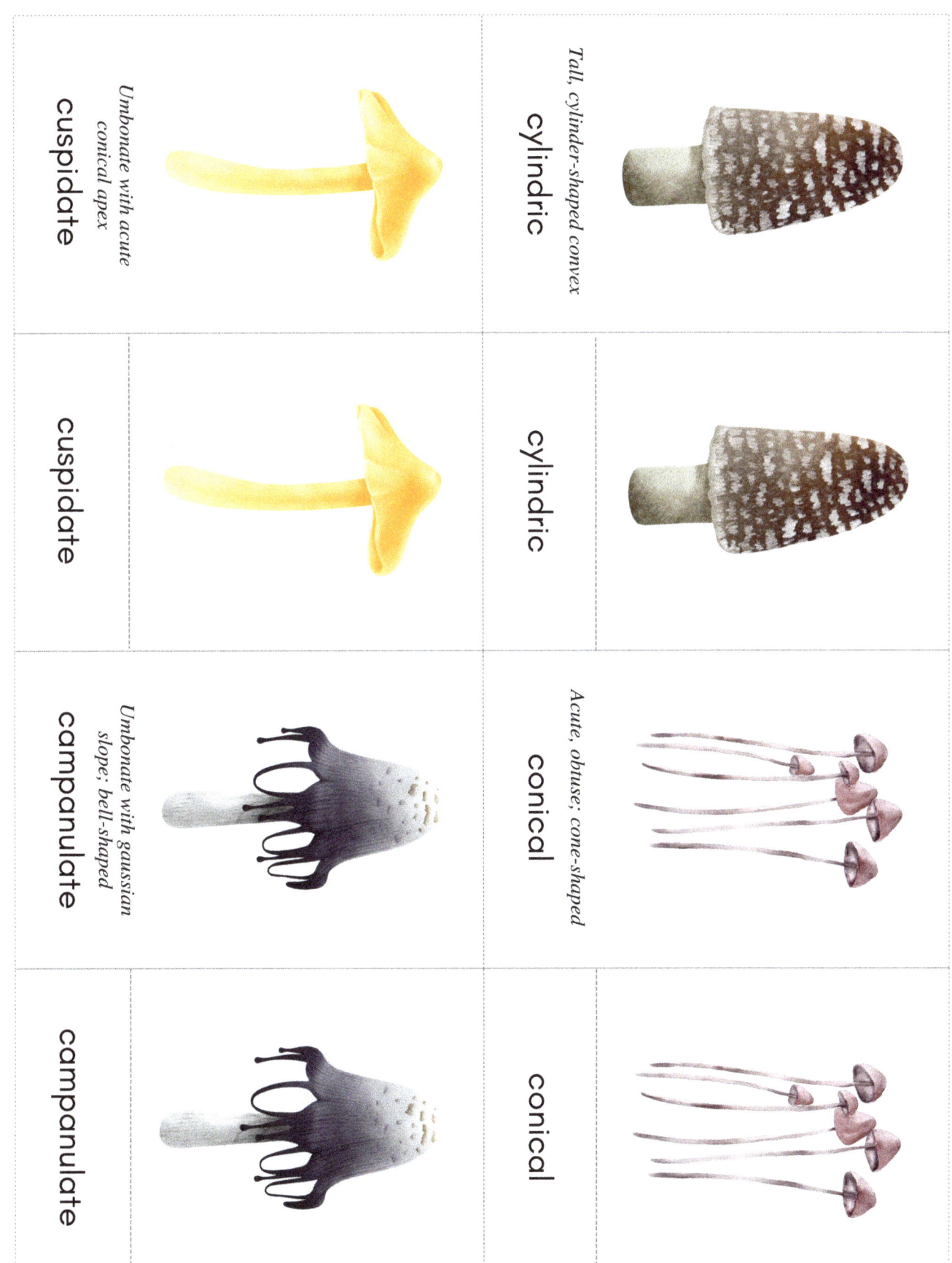

Mushroom Pileus Shape Cards

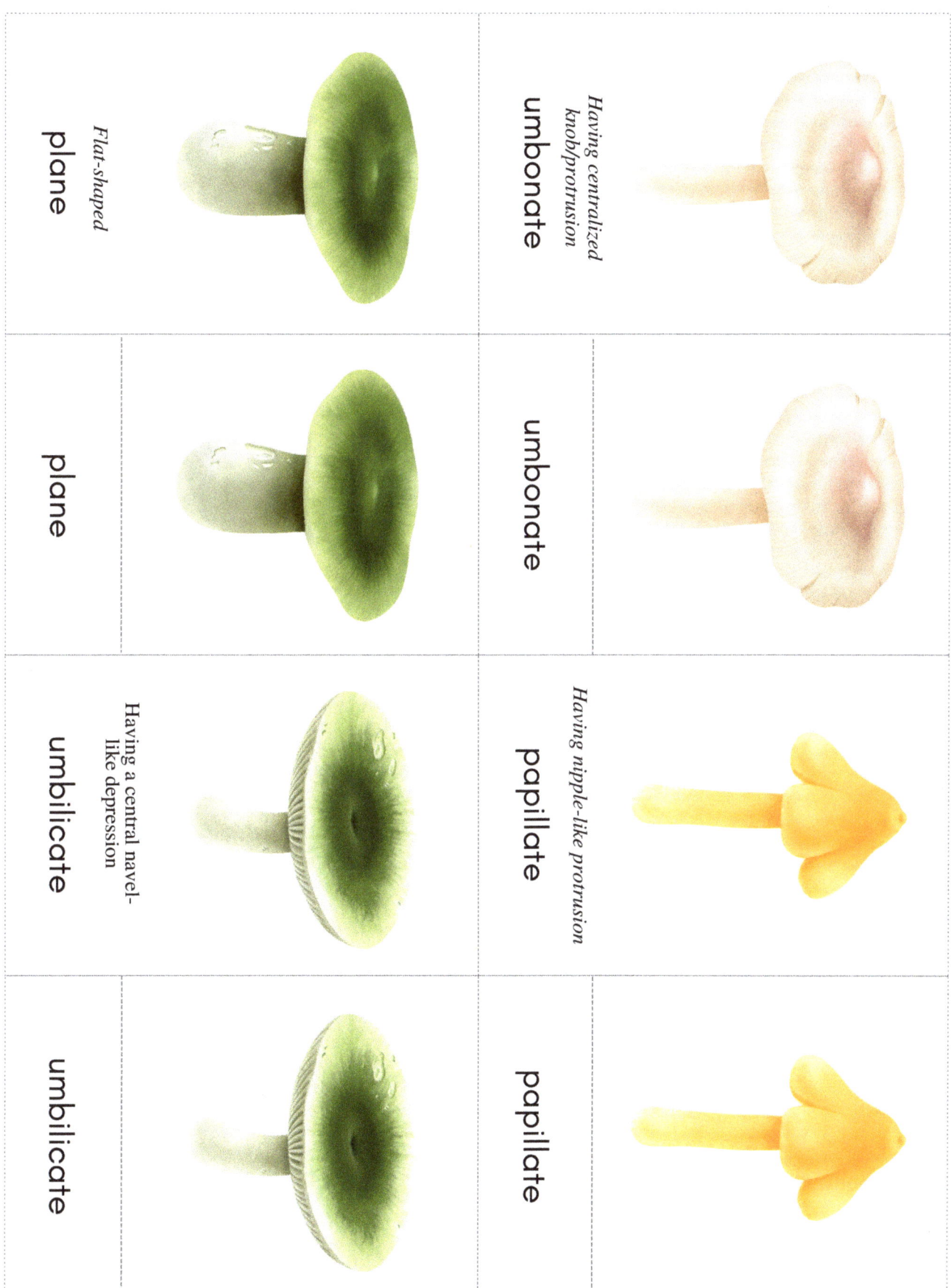

Mushroom Pileus Shape Cards

conchate — Bivalve shell appearance; oyster-shaped	**depressed** — Center is lower than cap margin; sauce-shaped
conchate	**depressed**
infundibuliform	**infundibuliform** — Deeply depressed; funnel-shaped

Confucius Coloring Page

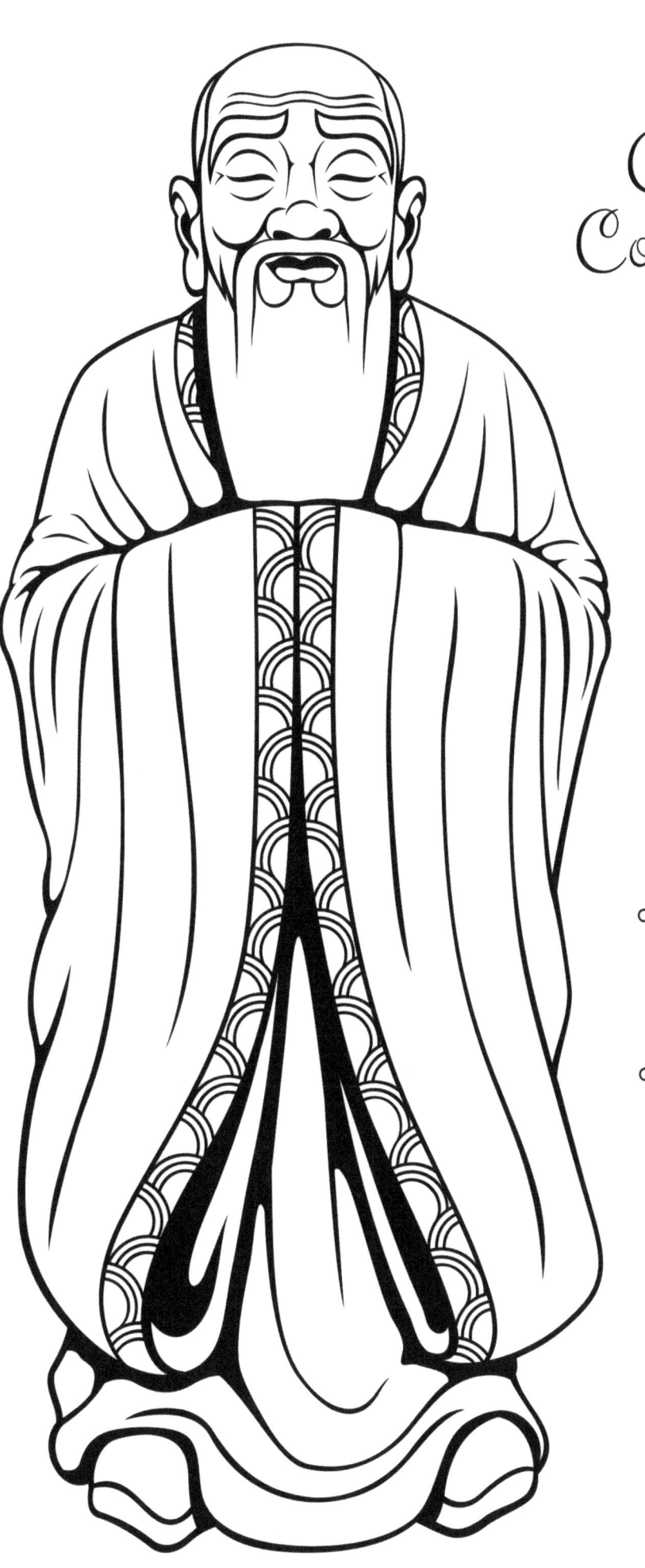

Confucius was a Chinese philosopher and politician during 551-479 BC. He is credited with the Golden Rule, *"Do not do unto others what you do not want done to yourself"*. Confucius is considered as one of the most important and influential individuals in human history.

MANDARIN LETTER TRACING

Materials
- Mandarin Phrase Cards
- Laminator (optional)
- Rice
- Red Food Coloring
- White Vinegar
- Sealable Bag
- Cooking Sheet
- Parchment Paper

Instructions

Mandarin Chinese is one of the major languages spoken and written in China. It is traditionally associated with China and the iconic lettering is highly recognizable around the world. This activity allows children to learn simple phrases in Mandarin Chinese, and work on early writing skills with fun sensory rice.

To dye rice, pour two cups of white rice into a zip-lock bag. Add one teaspoon of white vinegar and red food coloring until desired color is achieved. Seal bag and work color together until all rice is evenly coated. Spread onto parchment paper on cooking sheet and allow to dry. Laminate (optional) and cut out phrase cards.

Show child a phrase card. Have them trace the dry rice with a finger or utensil to create the symbols. Practice saying the phrases using the pronunciation guide.

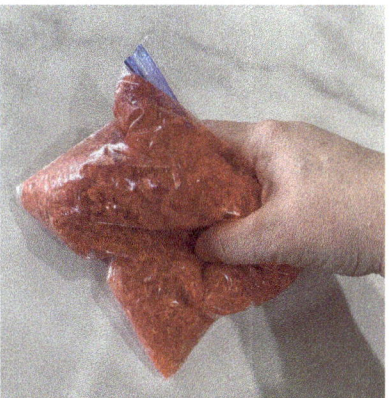

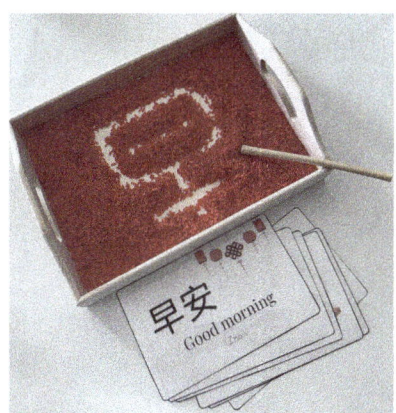

Mandarin Phrase Cards

你好

Hello

"Nee how"

别客气

You're welcome

"Bie kuh-chi"

Mandarin Phrase Cards

早安

Good morning

"Zao-un"

晚安

Goodnight

"One-un"

Mandarin Phrase Cards

多少

How Much?
"Dwuh shauw"

是 | 不是

Yes | No
"Sheh | Buh-sheh"

TANGRAM PUZZLE

Materials
- Tangram Puzzle
- Laminator (optional)
- Scissors
- Puzzle Cards

Instructions

The Tangram Puzzle is reputed to have been invented in China sometime around the late 18th century, and consists of seven flat polygons, called tans, which are put together to form shapes. The objective is to replicate a pattern.

Laminate the puzzle printout for additional durability. Cut out each colored shape so the pieces can be arranged back into square configuration.

Provide child with outline cards and have them rearrange the shapes to form the the design.

If the child cannot correctly recreate the design using the red outlines on the card, refer to the hints printed below the puzzle cutout for assistance.

Tangram Puzzle

Tangram Puzzle Cards

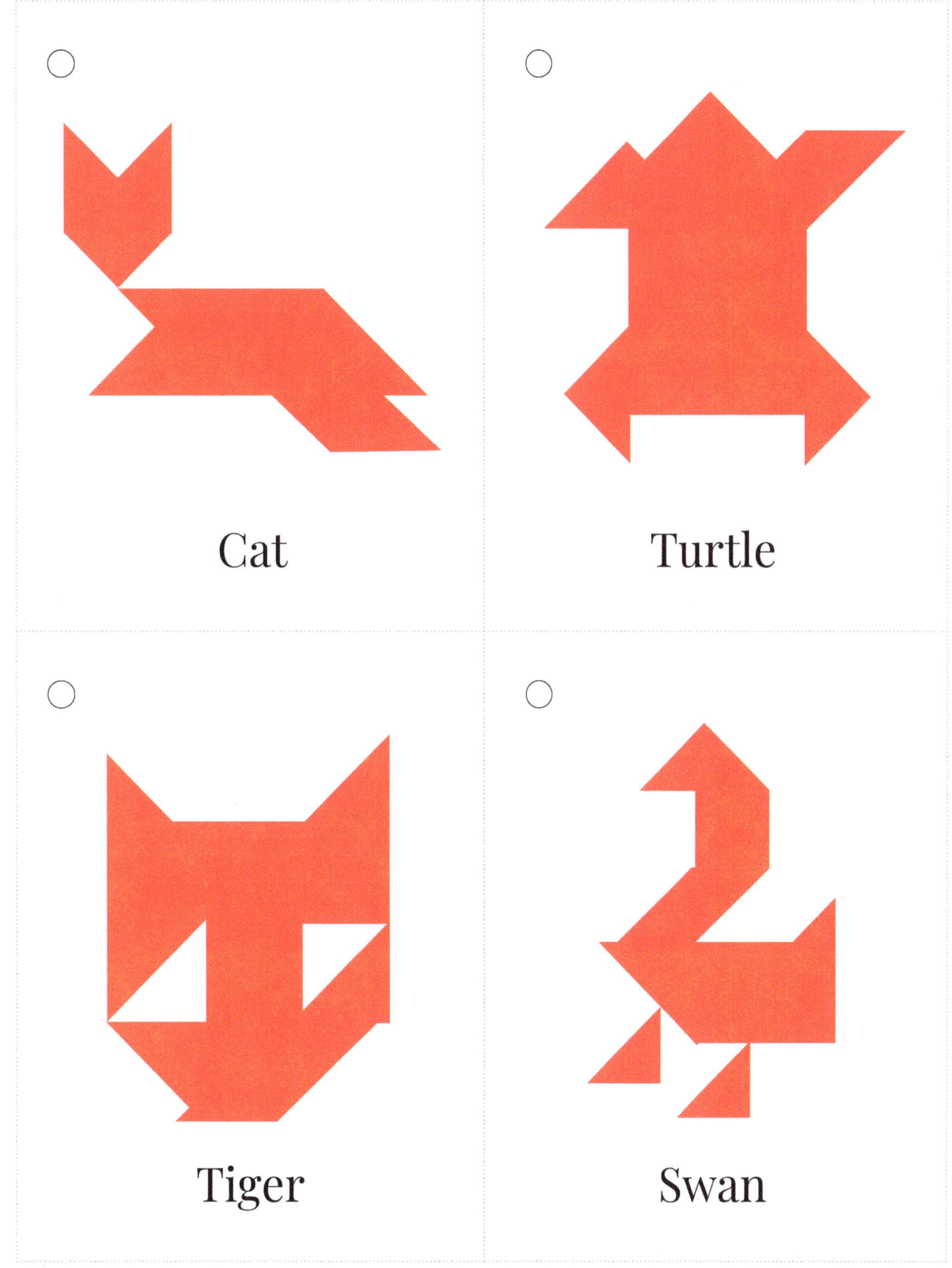

Tangram Puzzle Cards

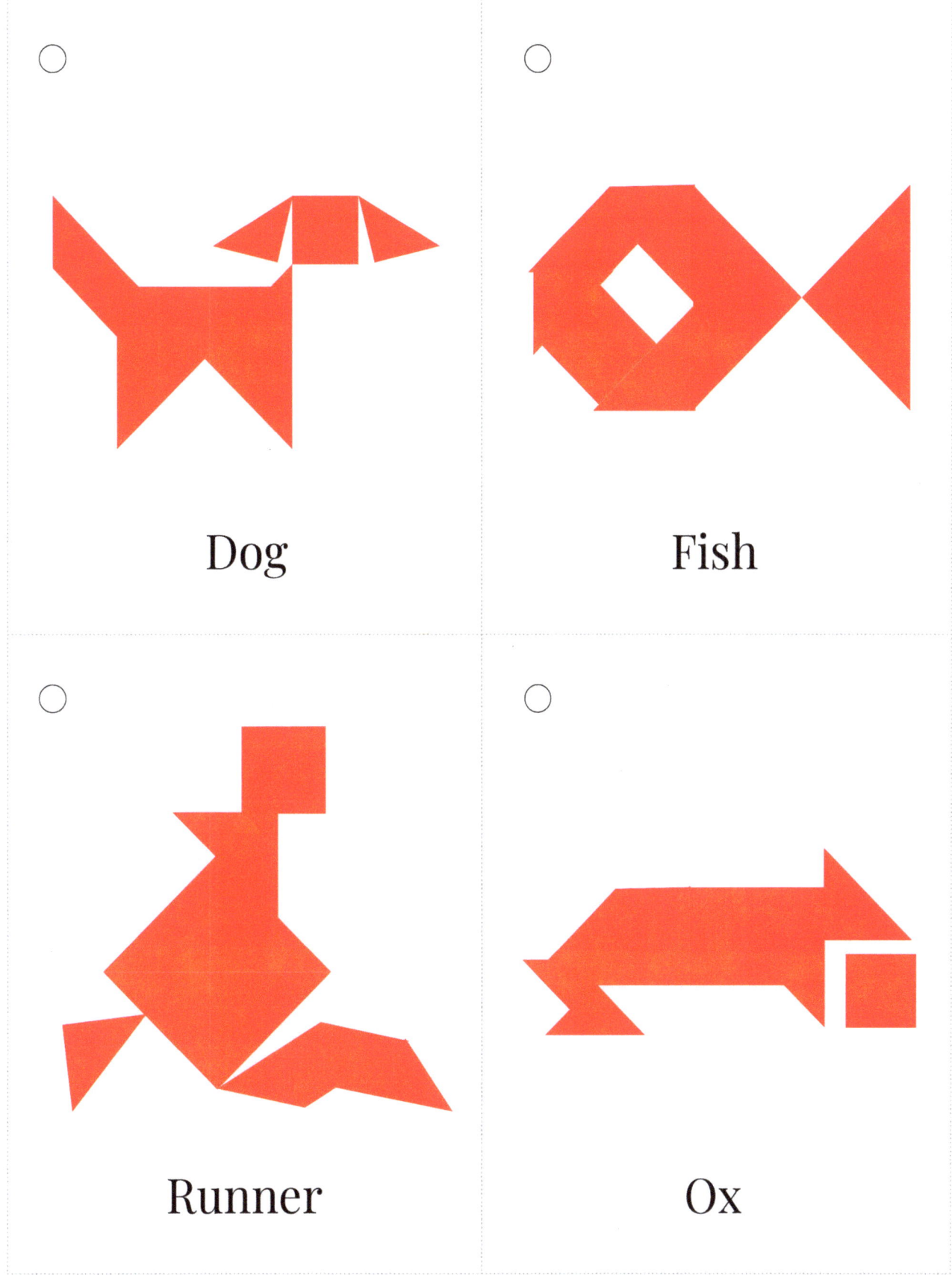

Counting Clip Cards

| 1 | 5 | 2 | 3 | 5 | 4 |

| 8 | 6 | 7 | 5 | 4 | 3 |

Counting Clip Cards

| 4 | 5 | 6 | 3 | 5 | 4 |

| 5 | 7 | 8 | 1 | 3 | 2 |

Counting Clip Cards

| 3 | 4 | 5 | 6 | 3 | 5 |

| 1 | 2 | 4 | 3 | 4 | 2 |

Savy Activities

Travel the world through the interactive learning activities of **Savy Activities**; these hands-on resources provide parents, caregivers and educators practical ways to teach children about the world around them. Each book features a country, location or time period where subjects such as geography, history, vocabulary, reading, language, science, mathematics, music and art come alive by engaging auditory, visual and kinesthetic learning styles.

All activity books include geography with applicable maps, landmarks and locations. Historical events and time periods are visually represented with full color posters and flashcards, if applicable. Each book includes a set of fun-fact cards, poster and flag, if applicable. Paper models allow children to create 3D creations of major landmarks and structures. All books include a life cycle and anatomy of a plant, animal or organic compound, with flashcards and 3-part cards featuring important structures applicable to the theme.

Children learn scientific principles through active experiments and activities. Traditional customs, festivals, toys, clothing and art are also explored. Each book includes an exclusive themed mini-story featuring historical events or traditional mythology and folklore to promote vocabulary and reading. Where applicable, world languages are introduced through engaging flashcards, posters and tracing work. Each country has been meticulously researched by interviewing native persons and/or personal travel experiences to ensure the authentic culture is fully explored.

Savy Activities utilizes concepts from multiple educational methods to create unique resources allowing children a tangible and enjoyable way to explore their world. The **Savy Activities** series should not be viewed as a curriculum, but rather complimentary thematic resources to enhance traditional education. Because the individual needs and knowledge of children varies within standardized grade levels, **Savy Activities** resources have the flexibility to be used with preschool learners through early to mid-elementary years. For younger learners, adult supervision and/or assistance may be needed and activities presented in a simplified version. For older learners, resources may be paired with additional content from other materials to meet learning outcomes.

Check out our other products and resources at **www.SavyActivities.com**

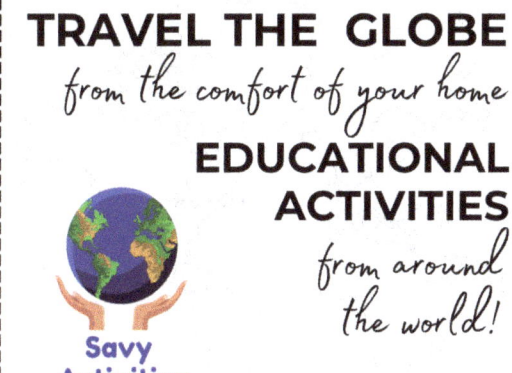

www.ingramcontent.com/pod-product-compliance
Lightning Source LLC
Chambersburg PA
CBHW060745240426

43665CB00054B/2996